Praise for Peter Selgin

The Inventors

· Finalist: Katharine Bakeless Nason Prize
· Finalist: Graywolf Press Prize for Nonfiction
· Finalist: AWP Award Series for Creative Nonfiction

In *The Inventors,* Peter Selgin unrolls the blueprint of his life, investigating how two men – his father and a charismatic middle-school teacher – helped create the man he is today. Lyrical, honest and (dare I say?) inventive, *The Inventors* is a deeply compelling meditation on how we make and remake ourselves throughout our lives – choice by choice, action by action, word by glorious, slippery word.

  GAYLE BRANDEIS, author of *The Book of Dead Birds*

The Inventors is a philosophical memoir that grapples with some of the questions regarding how we invent ourselves and how we in turn are invented by others, particularly by our mentors. Thanks to Selgin's autobiographical candor and the vivid details of his telling, these puzzles of identity seem as fresh, engaging, and befuddling as they were when they first bubbled to the surface of our thinking. A smart, tender, compelling book.

  BILLY COLLINS, author of *Aimless Love*

Peter Selgin writes brilliantly about our mindfulness and forgetting – the necessary inventions and reinventions that help us live. The lies of his father and his eighth-grade teacher inevitably enter into this intricate portrait of inner and outer selves. As he inhabits their action, talk, and thought, he teaches and fathers h[...]
cy, Mr. Selgin reminds h[...]
the genuine. In these re[...]
of our writers.

  CAROL FROST, a[...]

Peter Selgin's *The Inventors* is brilliant, brave, compelling, and inventive all at once. This is an intimately intimate rendering not just of Selgin's coming-of-age, but indeed of his rebirth into a new life of cognitive thought, of making sense of a perplexing world, of inventing out of blood and abstract ideas and hidden histories who, exactly, he is. This is an intelligent and moving book, a gorgeous book, an important book.

BRET LOTT, author of *Dead Low Tide*

Peter Selgin's *The Inventors* is a remarkable study in remembering, in empathy, and most of all in reckoning.

KYLE MINOR, author of *Praying Drunk*

Peter Selgin's intricately woven memoir, *The Inventors*, offers a unique, engaging, and occasionally startling examination of how childhood influences bend and shape us into being. Selgin's candor and intimacy bring to vivid life the Zen koan of how we become the people we become and how we somehow never really know who we are.

DINTY W. MOORE, author of *Between Panic & Desire*

I have never read anything like *The Inventors*, Peter Selgin's incomparable, brilliant, and achingly human memoir. With this deceptively simple story of the author's relationships with two self-invented figures – his father and an influential teacher – and with his own younger self – Selgin has produced a deep-core sample of the human condition. Like William Blake, he finds a whole world in a few grains of sand. He has shown, in language remarkably beautiful and accessible, how we are invented, by the people who profess to love and care for us and by our complicit selves. I was profoundly moved reading this book, by its deep intelligence, its constantly sweet, knowing humor, and the recognition in it of myself and everyone I have ever loved.

PETER NICHOLS, author of *The Rocks* and *A Voyage for Madmen*

Only a writer as gifted and insightful as Peter Selgin could have produced this deeply compelling story of two brilliant but extraordinarily deceitful men and the complicated relationships he shared with them. A superb work of memory that unfolds like a great suspense novel.

SIGRID NUNEZ, author of *Sempre Susan: A Memoir of Susan Sontag*

This story is about what we make and how we make it. Selves, lives, love stories, life stories, death stories. It is also the story of how creation and destruction are always the other side of each other. And like the lyrical language so gorgeously invented in this book that it nearly killed me, its meanings are endlessly in us. Writers live within language, and so in some ways, you might say we are at the epicenter.

LIDIA YUKNAVITCH, author of *The Chronology of Water* and *The Small Backs of Children*

Drowning Lessons

- Winner, 2007 Flannery O'Connor Award for Short Fiction
- Finalist: Iowa Short Fiction Award
- Finalist: Jefferson Press Prize
- Finalist: Ohio State University Press Prize

Thank goodness for Peter Selgin, who shares with us the mysteries of the human heart in this electric, revealing collection.

BENJAMIN PERCY, author of *Refresh, Refresh*

A stellar collection deserving recognition.

MELISSA PRITCHARD, author of *Late Bloomer*

Drowning Lessons is a book that deserves serious attention from all lovers of American short fiction.

JESS ROW, author of *The Train to Lo Wu*

Drowning Lessons is an extraordinary book; Selgin's writing creates a current that will carry readers farther than they would ever have expected and leave them on a new shore.

HANNAH TINTI, author of *Animal Crackers*

Life Goes to the Movies

- Finalist: AWP Award Series for the Novel
- Finalist: James Jones First Novel Fellowship

An utterly absorbing novel. A wonderful read.

MARGOT LIVESEY, author of *The House on Fortune Street*

From beginning to end, I kept imagining the funnels of smoke that surely must have risen from his keyboard as he wrote this potent, superbly crafted, and wonderfully ambitious novel.

DONALD RAY POLLOCK, author of *Knockemstiff*

Wonderfully innovative and elegantly crafted, *Life Goes to the Movies* brims with exuberance and wit.

FREDERICK REIKEN, author of *The Lost Legends of New Jersey*

[*Life Goes to the Movies* is] a riveting story, artfully constructed and told with wit, precision, and sensitivity.

JOANNA SCOTT, author of *Everybody Loves Somebody*

Confessions of a Left-Handed Man

· Finalist, William Saroyan International Prize

The quirky, intelligent memoir of an artist and fiction writer ... An engaging, original modern-day picaresque.

KIRKUS

Tawdry as [his] first love affair with literature may have been, how glad we are that Peter Selgin was tempted into it – and fell head over heels. Without such an addictive beginning, that boy may never have grown up to become a writer of such great substance.

NEW YORK JOURNAL OF BOOKS REVIEW

Selgin deftly balances humor and tenderness throughout these life-affirming confessions.

PUBLISHERS WEEKLY REVIEW

Peter Selgin is a born writer, capable of taking any subject and exploring it from a new angle with wit, grace, and erudition. He has a keen eye for the telling detail and a voice that is deeply personal, appealing, and wholly original. Fans of Selgin's fiction will know they are in for a treat, and those who are new to his work would do well to start with this marvelous memoir in essays, his finest writing yet.

OLIVER SACKS

Library of Congress
Cataloging-in-Publication Data

Selgin, Peter.
The inventors : a memoir /
by Peter Selgin.
pages cm
ISBN 978-0-9893604-7-0
(paperback)
1.   Selgin, Peter–Family.
2.   Teacher-student relationships–
     Biography.
3.   Authors, American–21st
     century–Biography.
PS3619.E463 Z46 2016
813/.6–dc23
2015030856

9
8
7
6
5
4
3
2

Hawthorne Books
& Literary Arts

2201 Northeast 23rd Avenue
3rd Floor
Portland, Oregon 97212
hawthornebooks.com

Printed in China

Set in Paperback

for Christopher Rowland

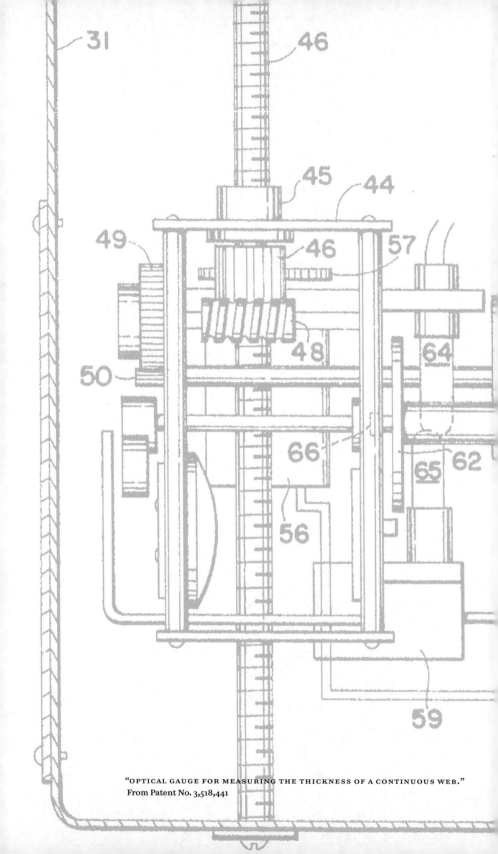

"OPTICAL GAUGE FOR MEASURING THE THICKNESS OF A CONTINUOUS WEB."
From Patent No. 3,518,441

The Inventors

a memoir
Peter Selgin

HAWTHORNE BOOKS & LITERARY ARTS
Portland, Oregon | MMXVI

Contents

Introduction
Lidia Yuknavitch

A "PROXIMITY FUZE," AN EVOLUTION OF THE "VARIABLE Time Fuze," was a fuze that automatically detonated an explosive device when the distance to a target became less than what had been programmed. Proximity fuzes were better than timed fuzes, which could go wrong in a myriad of ways. More precise. Less human error. Clusters of ground forces. Ships at sea. Enemy planes, various missiles, suspected ammunitions factories. Those were most often the targets.

And hearts.

At the heart of this book is a proximity fuze in the form of two men who entered and detonated Peter Selgin's life, leaving him to reconstitute a self from the pieces that were left. When we think about the people who come into and out of our lives, there are only a few – or less – who literally rearranged our DNA. You know what I'm talking about. Those people who, for whatever reason, detonated our realities. For Peter Selgin there were two men, one his father, who helped develop the proximity fuze, the other a teacher, who not only changed his life forever, but who had something in common with Selgin's father: they lied their way to selves.

I've always hated the word "lie." It has a bomb in its center. The bomb has a kind of morality trap inside of it. When we point to someone who "lied," we can more easily condemn them while feeling better about ourselves. And yet everyone I have ever met has lied. Sometime, somewhere. It's human to be bad at telling the truth. Truth is difficult and painful and often self-incriminating. I prefer the word "fiction." It allows for the fact that all of our truths – the stories we tell ourselves so that we can bear our own lives – are always already constructed. Our life fictions are compositions made from memory, and memory, as neuroscience now tells us, has no stable origin or pure access route.

I happen to be an expert on the topic of lies. My mother lied to me. My father lied to me. My family was a lie, my religion was a lie, husbands lied, teachers lied, friends and foes lied, the selves I was meant to step into – girlfriend, wife, mother – were all strange cultural fictions. Writers live within language, and so in some ways, you might say we are at the epicenter.

Peter Selgin's father was a brilliant man who participated in the extraordinary inventions but also the death sciences that culminated in the atomic bombs used on Hiroshima and Nagasaki. In order to forge a self he could live with, he fictionalized his own past. And because life is always bringing the same trials back around to us in different forms, later in his life Peter Selgin would meet another man, a teacher whose fictions recreated a self that might rise above the human wrongs he'd committed. Peter writes from within the epicenter of each.

This story is about what we make and how we make it: selves, lives, love stories, life stories, death stories. It is also the story of how creation and destruction are always the other side of each other, and – like the lyric language so gorgeously invented in this book that it nearly killed me – its meanings are endlessly in us. It's a book about how we do and do not survive our twin forms of being: the selves we live, and the stories of those selves we endlessly recreate. And there is something at the heart of the story that I did not expect to find.

Hope.

slab of fudge at its center, a frozen masterpiece. It helped dull the ache of surrendering Jill Butterworth to the water and other boys.

Then came the Saturday toward the end of that summer when two disasters struck. First, while conducting your reconnaissance of the park, you caught Jill kissing Harvey Keebler – the same Harvey Keebler whose mother your brother would inadvertently tell to go fuck herself – behind one of the two floats.

In a state of grief you approached the Good Humor man and asked for a Banana Split, to be told that it was no longer, that it had been a summer special, that something repulsive to do with strawberries had taken its place. It took every last measure of your will to keep from grasping the Good Humor man by his spanking white uniform lapels and sullying them with salty tears.

* * *

SOME TIME BETWEEN HALLOWEEN AND THANKSGIVING you arrived at the carriage house to find a girl's green Schwinn parked by the blue door. You heard voices inside. With an ear pressed to the door you heard the words "quotidian" and "sanctimonious" and identified one of the voices as that of Vivian Y., who shared the teacher's special class with you. Vivian wrote and recited impenetrable (at least by you) poems stuffed with words that fell well beyond your (admittedly restricted) vocabulary. Vivian was well read and articulate and tended to monopolize class discussions. Thanks partly to this but mainly because she'd made it so abundantly clear that she had no interest whatsoever in you, you found her intriguing, albeit annoyingly so.

It was a cloudy day. The murky atmosphere turned everything gray – the carriage house's clapboards, the roof shingles, even the blue door. From inside the cottage you heard a burst of feminine laughter. Feeling instantly jealous you knocked extra loudly on the blue door. Through it you heard the teacher's voice:

Come in, Peter.

You entered to find the teacher and Vivian seated at the table. You saw the pottery teacups and chess pieces scattered around the chessboard. As you took off your sneakers Vivian sat there in a desultory air. She didn't look at all happy to see you. Vivian had long straight brown hair that she parted in the middle and that fell two thirds of the way down her slim back. Her forehead was high, her chin pointy, her nose narrow and straight down to its tip, where it curved suddenly up into a little ball – like (you thought scornfully) the meatballs in a can of Progresso Chickarina soup.

Hey, Vivian, you said with forced cheer.

Hey, she responded with unalloyed indifference.

The teacher asked you if you wanted tea. Yes, you said, that would be lovely. As you said the word "lovely" you turned in time to catch Vivian's look of disgust. You tossed her a smirk and crossed to the kitchen area, where you pretended to search for the teacup you always used, one with a little fish design etched into the clay and fired with a delicate cuprous oxide glaze, though you had already seen the cup on the table and knew that Vivian had been using it.

Have you seen my cup? you asked, searching, or pretending to search, for it. You know, the one with the fish design on it? I could swear I put it back last time I used it.

You extended this burlesque for a few more minutes, moving cups and other items in the cabinet. Then: Oh, wait, there it is on the table. Were you using my cup, Vivian? No, no, no, that's perfectly okay; I'll get another.

You took another cup and sat down. That's when you noticed all the black chess pieces gathered on Vivian's side of the table, with the solitary black king on the chessboard surrounded by white pieces. The teacher always played Black. Vivian had beaten the teacher at chess – something you had attempted many times but never managed to do. For this alone you wished her dead and in hell.

Been playing chess, I see, you observed.

Yes, said Vivian contemptuously. We were playing chess.

It's a challenging game, isn't it? You touched one of the pieces.

Yes, said Vivian, rolling not her eyes but her voice. Quite challenging.

Have you tried the Queen's Gambit? Or the King's Indian Attack?

You made awkward chess chatter for a while, until finally Vivian excused herself, saying that she had "a ton" of homework to do.

Gee, that's too bad. Anything I can possibly help you with?

Thanks, but no, Vivian – who by then was already putting her red vinyl boots on – replied. Before leaving she gave the teacher a peck on the cheek, balancing herself on the toe of one of the boots as she did so. Then without looking at you she went out the door, got on her Schwinn, and pedaled away into the gray afternoon.

You waited a moment or two before saying to the teacher, as you twirled the vanquished black king:

Too bad I didn't get here any sooner. I might have spared you the agony of defeat.

She's very good, the teacher replied while doing dishes.

At what?

Don't be a jerk.

If you ask me I'd say she's got a crush on you.

I didn't ask. Anyway Vivian's a lovely woman.

A woman?

That's right.

What makes her a woman, other than the fact that she swallowed a thesaurus?

She acts like a woman.

Oh? What about me? Do I act like a man?

Sometimes.

When don't I act like one?

Right now, for instance.

Why? What did I do?

A man doesn't ask other people whether or not he acts like a man.

You watched glumly as the teacher washed, dried, and put away plates and silverware. He wore the gray sweatshirt with OXFORD on it.

You don't seem to like Vivian very much, he said.

I don't.

Why don't you?

Because – she's just not my type.

Really? What's your type?

None of your business.

You do like girls, don't you?

What's that supposed to mean? Of course I like girls!

It was just a question. No need to get defensive.

I'm not being defensive. Who says I'm being defensive?

The teacher laughed.

What are you laughing about? What's so damn funny?

He kept on laughing. You said *cut it out!* – which made him laugh harder. *Shut up!* you said, and he laughed harder still. The more you tried to get him to stop, the harder the teacher laughed, until his face was red and tears fell from his eyes.

That's when you lunged. Together you and the teacher rolled across the blue floorboards, wrestling, with the teacher still laughing and you saying *Shut the hell up, goddammit!* You'd wrestled before – with George, of course, and in phys ed, with Coach Hunt slapping the matt. But this was much more pleasurable. The teacher's arms were stronger, his legs were longer. It took him less than a minute to pin you, his big hands pressing your shoulders down, holding them to the blue floorboards, his chest heaving, his lips sparkling with saliva, his blond hair hanging over his face, the round lenses of his glasses reflecting twin flames from a candle on the table.

The wide floorboards reminded you of ocean waves as you lay there, stretched out and out of breath, snickering, feeling happy – as happy or even happier than you'd ever felt before in your whole life.

Dingleberry! you said, laughing.

Smelly cheeser! said the teacher.

THE WIDE-PLANKED BLUE FLOORBOARDS. THE HORSEY *smell of that tea-soaked Japanese table. The feeling that you'd not just entered the home of your teacher but been initiated into a new world filled with its own intrigues, mysteries, its own secret language and codes. A heady experience for a thirteen-year-old boy. And it wasn't only the experience of a world but of falling in love for the first real time with someone who – in his way – could return that love, who made you feel worthy and special.*

* * *

FOR YEARS I'VE TRIED TO WRITE ABOUT THE TEACHER, *to make our relationship comprehensible – as opposed to classifiable or categorical – to disinterested parties. Glib phrases like "teacher's pet" and "closet case" don't do it justice – not in my estimation, an estimation that (some would say) is prejudiced, that can't or won't accept that what was once so charged with meaning, loftiness, and intensity can be reduced to banalities. Even if that happens to be the case, even if I was as naive as my youthful days were long, still, as with any love story, something irreducible exists at its core, the beauty of which lies in the fact that it can't be properly understood or appreciated by anyone outside of it.*

 The teacher himself tried to warn me about this back when we were still in Bethel. "They [other people] will never understand what you and I have," he said. "They can't understand because they've never had anything like it themselves. Their misfortune could be our undoing,

Peter, since what people can't understand they distrust, and what they distrust they tend to destroy. They'll turn it into something they can understand, something vulgar, banal, worthy of gossip and intrigue. They'll drag it down to earth. They'll bury it alive."

* * *

I SIT ON MY DOCK WATCHING THE SUNSET. WE GET THE *most fabulous sunsets here. Over the treetops across the water the sky burns orange, rose, and pink. I can barely see the pages of my notebook. In more ways than one I'm writing in the dark. It stands to reason. Exhuming the past, digging up its corpse, is a job best undertaken by night.*

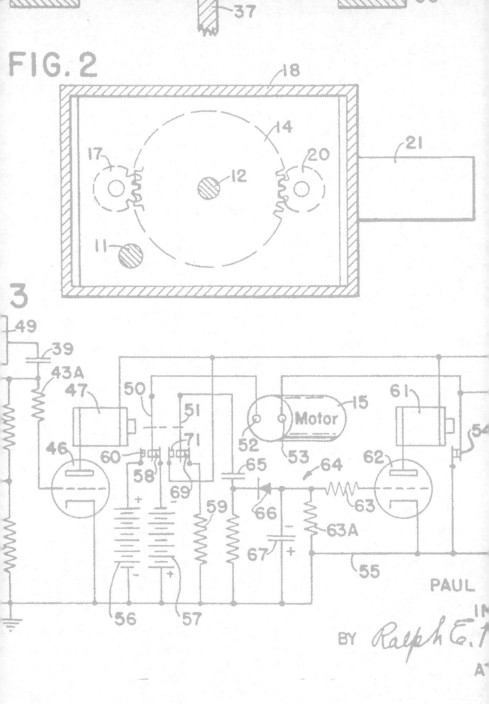

FIG. 2

United States Patent No. 3,423,595: "DISTANCE MEASURING MEANS USING LIGHT BEAMS." Patented January 21, 1969.

VIII.
Christmas Dinner
Bethel, Connecticut, 1970

IT WAS YOUR MOTHER'S IDEA TO HAVE THE TEACHER OVER on Christmas Eve. The day before, a blizzard dropped fifteen inches of snow on the town. You spent the morning shoveling walkways, including the one to the front door (so rarely used it stuck to the jamb). You were glad to have something to keep you busy. You were as eager about this Christmas Eve as on previous Christmas mornings you'd been anxious over the prospect of a mound of gifts glittering under a tree ablaze with lights.

After shoveling all the walks, while your brother read a book, you assembled and trimmed the Christmas tree. You wanted a real Christmas tree that year, as you'd wanted a real Christmas tree the year before and the one before that.

Your mother refused. She didn't want pine needles all over the place.

And so you dragged the fake Christmas tree in its battered cardboard box up from its storage place under the basement stairs, and spent the next half-hour attaching fake branches to the fake trunk, and another hour trimming it, stringing bulbs and lights and tinsel, stopping now and then to assess the result only to find it spurious. A Christmas tree in the Selgin household, that den of heathens, made as little sense as a screen door on a submarine. Who did you think you were you fooling?

Oh, well, it was better than no Christmas tree at all.

You strung more colored lights around the barrel hedges in the yard and in a spiral around the lamppost rising from one of them. You vacuumed, made the beds (yours and your brother's), put the extenders into the dining table and covered it with the red tablecloth and then with another tablecloth made of white lace before setting it with the fancy yellow china your mother kept in a bottom cupboard. You jammed tapered red candles into two matching sterling candleholders, adorned them with sprigs of plastic holly, and positioned one at each end of the table.

In the laundry room you gave the dog a bath so she wouldn't smell so bad.

BY THEN IT was almost five o'clock. Mr. Peck, the husband of your mother's best friend before she died of a brain aneurysm, had already arrived. In the breakfast nook where he'd seated himself, he spoke to your mother, who wore a green gown while preparing appetizers at the counter with her back to him. Since his wife's passing Mr. Peck had been coming over regularly and usually unannounced for lunch and dinner, and sometimes even for breakfast. He wouldn't bother to knock. He'd clomp into the kitchen in the heavy tan brogans he wore to the construction sites he owned, depositing dry noodles of mud on the floor that Pa'al would eat or try to. He'd plant himself in the breakfast nook, where, while guzzling your mother's coffee (that he'd criticize for being too weak), he'd complain about the latest tax increase or deadbeat tenant occupying one of his rental properties.

In place of his brogans that evening, Mr. Peck wore a clean plaid shirt and leather shoes and a yellow scarf that he hadn't taken off yet.

Hey, there, Mr. Peck, you said, greeting him in a brocade vest reminiscent of those worn by James West. You wore it with a pair of cowboy boots, black and polished to a polar glare.

Fancy duds, Mr. Peck observed, sizing you up and down, pursing his lower lip that protruded from his face like a toadstool. His bald head reflected the kitchen light.

You helped your mother with the antipasti, platters laden with cured meats, cheeses, dips, spreads, several kinds of olives, deviled eggs, *prosciutto e melone,* and your favorite, *peperona-ta* – sliced roasted peppers in olive oil with vinegar and garlic.

HAVING LEFT WORK and walked up the driveway from his laboratory, your father sat in his rocking chair with his German dictionary in his lap. George lay sprawled on the carpet watching the *Mr. Magoo Christmas Special* while reading a book about undersea exploration. He wore his pajamas; he'd been wearing them all day, you realized as you stood there holding a tray of antipasti. The teacher was coming over and look at him. Impious scubadiving bookworm! Goodfornothing slob! You wanted to kick him in the rump, but resisted, knowing it would only start a war. Instead, having put the antipasti tray down on the coffee table, you announced:

Mr. Peck's here.

George didn't budge.

Is he now? said your father. Well, I suppose I should go say hello.

Having marked the page in his German dictionary and put it next to the lamp on his reading table, with a deep existential sigh, your papa rose stiffly from his chair. Wearing a relatively clean pair of what he called "trousers" and the paisley cardigan you'd given him last Christmas he made his way to the kitchen.

You said to your brother:

You gonna watch TV all night?

George watched TV.

We've got company, in case you haven't noticed.

Mr. Magoo encountered Jacob Marley's chain-wrapped ghost.

Dingleberry, you said.

BACK IN THE kitchen you cracked two trays of ice into the stainless bucket and opened two bottles of wine, one red, one white. Your mother opened the oven and tested the turkey with a fork. As you turned the corkscrew in a bottle you looked up at the clock. A quarter after six. The invitation had been for six o'clock.

The teacher didn't have a car. He'd be coming by foot. When

you asked him if he wanted a ride, he declined. I don't mind walking, he said. Now with a foot of snow on the roads and more snow falling you wondered if he'd changed his mind. Since he had no telephone, you couldn't call the teacher to find out, nor could he phone you.

Your guest is late, said Mr. Peck.

He'll be here, you said.

Must be some kind of nut, walking in weather like this.

Be nice, Erb, your mother said, pronouncing Mr. Peck's name so it sounded like something you sprinkled into soups. Bad that it goes we eat a bit later, she said.

Doesn't this teacher of yours drive? Mr. Peck wondered.

He doesn't have a car, you submitted proudly.

I'll be damned – no car, your father said with admiration. I wish I could get away with that. I much prefer walking or riding my bicycle.

I enjoy walking, too, said Mr. Peck, but not in weather like this.

Suum cuique, your father said.

What's that mean?

To each his own.

You looked up at the clock again. Twenty after six. You were still looking at the clock when George entered the kitchen. He wore a long-sleeved dress shirt patterned with loud purple grapevines.

Season's greetings, said Mr. Peck, shaking his hand.

You look like a hippy, you remarked.

I see you raided Liberace's wardrobe, your brother said. That vest come with a dimmer switch?

Screw you.

Brotherly love, Mr. Peck observed.

THROUGH THE SWINGING doors you entered the dining room where you sat in the darkness by the bay window watching snowflakes fall around the lamp that you'd decorated with colored lights. Any moment now, you told yourself, the teacher will walk up the driveway. I'll see him walking, his face lit by the lamp, the shoulders of his coat powdered with snow. It seemed impossible to you, yet it was inevitable. All of the conditions had been met, all forces set in motion. You peered out the window, your breath fogging the glass, asking yourself: *Will he really come?*

Then you saw him coming up the steep slope, hunched over, walking into the light cast by the lamp. It lit up his breaths and highlighted the snowflakes falling around him. You waited for him to turn up the sidewalk you'd shoveled. Instead, he continued to the back of the house, where a second floodlight shined from the eave of the garage. When he broached it Pa'al started barking.

Your mother yelled:

Is *ere!*

You hurried back into the kitchen. The door buzzer sounded. There was the usual pandemonium as Pa'al jumped and mewled and tried to lick the teacher's face.

Okay, okay, he said, petting her, averting his mouth. I take it this is Pa'al?

Worst behaved dog in the universe, George said

The teacher wiped and kicked the snow off his boots in the tiny mudroom that your mother called the "little porch." He took off his scarf. Mr. Peck and your father stood in the nook. You and George stood in the center of the kitchen. Your mother stood by her antique black Chambers stove. The teacher took off his hat and gloves.

Thanks, he said, handing them to you along with his scarf.

You mother told you to take the teacher's "jacket" – meaning his winter coat – too. Under it the teacher wore a dull green corduroy sport coat with a pale yellow shirt and a striped necktie. You'd never seen him in a tie before.

The men having introduced themselves, the teacher turned to your mother.

Mrs. Selgin. He offered his hand.

Pinuccia. She hugged and kissed his cheek.

Pinuccia?

Is short for Giuseppina. *Giuseppantonia, Giuseppina, Pina, Pinuccia.* She looked him over. *Ma sei cosi giovane! E anche un bell'uomo.*

What did she say? the teacher asked.

She says you're good-looking, you answered. My mother's a shameless flirt. You should see her flirting with the UPS guy.

Ma va, said your mother.

Mr. Peck's laugh was more of a snort.

The teacher gave your mother a bottle. Spice wine, he said. From the Brotherhood Winery. Then to you: Your mother's not exactly decrepit herself.

Eh? your mother said.

It's a compliment, Mom. He's complimenting you.

Someone call a translator, said Mr. Peck. It's like the United Nations in here.

The United Nations, that's a good one, said your father.

Please, everyone sit down. No make compliment!

YOU CARRIED THE teacher's things to the closet by the front door, which, when opened, exhaled a breath of musty cold air, then returned to the kitchen where everyone stood talking still. You watched them, enjoying how they all seemed to be getting along, proud of your role in having engineered this event.

Your mother had you pour the teacher some wine. You poured yourself half a glass, too, and used it to wash down a deviled egg (your mother made very good deviled eggs). While swallowing the deviled egg you couldn't help noticing, as the teacher stood next to your father, the differences between them. Your father was at least four inches shorter than the teacher, the remaining strands of hair on his head gray, brushed back from a sloping forehead covered with wrinkles and spattered with liver spots, with fuzzy white tufts of hair sprouting from his ears. The teacher's hair was golden and shiny. It reflected the kitchen lights. His shoulders were broader, his chest bigger, his stomach flatter. Your father had a paunch.

Then there were the teacher's hands, one holding his wine

glass, the other propped on the counter next to the deviled eggs. They couldn't have been less like your father's. They were larger, with long fingers, their nails trimmed square and clean. Your father's hands were small, their fingers stubby, dark and wrinkled, with quarter-moons of grime under the nails: the hands he curved over the lathe's spinning chuck, the hands you once held in such high esteem.

You listened to the teacher and your father talking. They were discussing England.

Peter tells me you went to Oxford. Ah, those dreamy spires!

I understand that you're very fond of England yourself, Mr. Selgin.

Please, call me Paul. It's true, your father said, I've always been. Since I was a boy. What I like most about the English is their wit. Italians are funny. Americans like cracking jokes. Whereas the English are witty. They say funny things without meaning to be funny. That's the difference. It's why you'll rarely hear an Englishman laugh at his own joke. He's not joking, not in the least. He's being quite serious. (Your father's Oxbridge accent had grown thicker.) Whereas Americans are *always* laughing at their own jokes. Have you noticed?

Mr. Peck gave a look that said, *There goes that egocentric father of yours.* It hadn't been long since the time when, sipping your mother's weak coffee with the screen door freshly slammed behind him and your father headed to work, he remarked:

There goes the most egocentric human being I ever expect to encounter in my entire life.

THE PARTY MOVED to the living room. George carried the dish of deviled eggs. You followed with the *prociutto e melone.* The fake Christmas tree blazed. Walter Cronkite's avuncular face filled the TV screen. Your mother had you turn it off. She sat on the sofa. Your father reclaimed his rocking chair. Mr. Peck sat on the upholstered chair. The teacher was about to sit on the ottoman but your mother insisted that he keep her company on the sofa, where Pa'al had taken up her usual position, her dull gold muzzle jutting over its edge, a perfect match for the threadbare upholstery. Mr. Peck ate another deviled egg. He said to the teacher:

So how are you finding Bethel?

Before the teacher could answer, Nonnie entered. She wore her veiled cocktail hat and had her wooden cane. Along with everyone your father greeted her, but with a faint malicious glint in his eyes. Mr. Peck stood again, this time to offer her his chair, moving to one of the folding chairs you'd brought in from the enclosed unheated porch.

You and George were still standing, biding your time, letting the grown-ups talk for a while before reducing the discussion to sarcasm, insults, and brutal jokes.

Che cosa succede? Nonnie asked.

Niente, Nonna, said your mother.

Mr. Peck turned to the teacher.

I take it you haven't been teaching long. You can't be much over twenty.

I'm twenty-four.

I once taught, said your father. At the Polytechnic Institute in Brooklyn. It was during the Depression. I couldn't get a job. The job recruiting officer said, You don't want to *teach*, do you? I rather enjoyed it, as a matter of fact.

Mr. Peck pursed his toadstool lip.

You watched as they went on talking. You didn't pay attention to what they said so much as to the expressions on their faces, how they looked at each other and smiled and listened with mutual interest and pleasure. It delighted you. The two men who meant the most to you – your father and the teacher – getting along like … not like brothers (they were too far apart in age for that). More like father and son.

The discussion turned to books.

Have you read Proust? your father asked.

Yes, have you?

Your father shook his head. I never finished it. I'm afraid

I can't stomach his precious affectations. His metaphors are all wrong. I'll give you an example. At one point Proust writes something to the effect that the leaves of a tree give off a scent when "allowed to" by the rain, *"la parfum que les feuilles laissent s'échapper avec les dernières gouttes de pluie,"* something like that. It makes no sense. Not if you think about it. The rain doesn't "allow" or "permit" the leaves to emit anything. That sort of language just doesn't work, not for me, anyway.

You're being awfully hard on Proust, the teacher said.

Well – why shouldn't I be?

A novel isn't an electronic instrument. It's a work of art. Poetic language doesn't have to answer to logic, at least not always.

Why shouldn't it have to? If I wire a circuit incorrectly, if I replace a capacitor with a resistor, it simply doesn't work. There's no two ways about it. Proust's writing doesn't work for me. But then what do I know? I'm an engineer.

Am I dreaming, said Mr. Peck, turning to you and your brother, or did your father just utter something relatively modest?

Che cosa succede? Nonnie said.

Stronzo, your father said under his breath.

Paolo! your mother scolded him.

What's that? asked the teacher.

Niente, Nonna, your mother said. *Non succede niente.*

Mr. Peck snorted.

IN THE DINING room you pulled back your grandmother's chair. Your mother sat – when she sat at all – by the swinging door to the kitchen. Your father sat at the far end of the table by the window. Mr. Peck carved the turkey, sharpening the knife flamboyantly on the steel first, then noting as he carved (his lower lip quivering along with the knife in his hand) that the drippings were still pink.

You've undercooked the damn bird, he said.

(When displeased your mother made puffing sounds. She made one now.)

You poured eggnog into your wine glass. As Mr. Peck went

on carving, your father recited a limerick – the one about the epicurean dining at Crewe who found a mouse in his stew, or the Lady from Trent whose nose was so horribly bent, or the one from Ride who ate too many apples and died. When you begged him to stop he broke into titters.

With everyone's plate filled your mother drank her wine and sat back and told stories about her Italian childhood, including the one about the time Mussolini kissed her. She'd been captain of her school district's volleyball team, which had won first place in the *Pala al Volo Campionana Nationale.* Having draped the medal over her, when she faced him, Il Duce (*"allowasan"* – "all of a sudden") kissed her.

On de cheek, de *lef* one, your mother said. Three years later, presented with the opportunity to throw stones at the fascist leader's corpse, she refused.

How dey expek me to trow stone at him when ee *kiss* me? I say to dem, *Ma va al diavolo!*

THE SUBJECT OF war having thus been broached, Mr. Peck asked the teacher his views on Vietnam.

Please, no let talk politic, said your mother.

You knew this moment was coming. You'd predicted it, had even looked forward to it with a mixture of curiosity and fear. You'd heard Mr. Peck and your pacifist father argue enough to know where Mr. Peck stood on the subject. And though he hadn't said it in so many words, you knew the teacher was against the war. You'd known it since the day he brought a stack of *New York Times* to class.

I assume you've all heard of the war, he said, handing a copy to each student. *Well, now you can read about it. One day you may be doing a lot more than reading.*

Days later, the teacher showed the class a short, black-and-white movie. It showed a lone soldier walking along a deserted beach. He stops to feed a gull a piece of chocolate from his mess kit. A shot rings out. The rest of the film shows the soldier falling in slow motion to the ground. His helmet rolls away in the sand. A student informed his parents, who complained to the administration (so the teacher, who kept nothing from you, told you during one of your visits).

Mr. Peck looked at the teacher, who chewed his food for a while before responding quietly: We shouldn't be there.

Why not?

Your mother changed the subject. What you tink of de new bool? she said.

Papa: *Bool?* What's a bool?

Mom: De one de town want to build.

George: The indoor pool.

Papa: Oh, a *pool.*

Mr. Peck: It's a boondoggle. We've already got a pool.

George: He means the town park.

You: Meckhauer.

George: That mud hole!

Mr. Peck: This town needs an indoor pool like it needs a canal.

Papa: A man, a plan, a canal: Panama.

Nonnie: *Che cosa succede?*

Papa: Personally, I'd vote for a trolley system. Wouldn't that be a good thing? A system of little yellow streetcars that could take people back and forth into town.

George: We could also build an Eiffel Tower. Or a landing field for a dirigible.

Mr. Peck: Makes as much sense as an indoor pool.

You: You say so cuz you don't like to swim!

George: Mr. Peck doesn't know *how* to swim.

Papa: No wonder he doesn't like it!

Nonnie: *Che cosa succede?*

Mom: *Niente, Nonna, niente.*

Mr. Peck: Nor do I have any inclination to learn.

George: It beats drowning.

Mr. Peck: From my perspective the difference is purely semantic. If people want to swim let them do it on their own dime.

You: Mr. Peck hates anything to do with water. He doesn't even take baths.

Mr. Peck: I prefer to shower. Saves water.

Teacher: Is it true, Mrs. Selgin?

Mom: Please, call me Pinuccia. Is what true?

Teacher: Did you really kiss Mussolini?

Mom: No, ee kiss *me!*

Mr. Peck: And a couple years later they strung him and his wife up in the plaza and threw stones at them. See what kissing Pinuccia will get you?

Mom: *Ma va – cretino!*

AS YOUR MOTHER poured the coffee and served the zabaglione, your father launched into his usual tirade about the failure of American industrial designers to arrive at an intelligent design for a creamer that wouldn't spill like the one from the silver service, which dribbled all over the table when your father put cream in his coffee, how such vessels with their enormous but purposeless (if not altogether contraindicated) spouts were not only a nuisance but contemptible, especially when one considered how simple it would be to design a vessel that would pour properly, how all that would be required is a simple notch, that's all, a notch such as could be made with the tip of a round file on the lip of the vessel, a simple unelaborated notch on top of an enclosed cylinder, nothing more, and voila, you would have a vessel that would pour perfectly every time, without spilling a drop. Instead they had to contrive some inefficient monstrosity with an enormous useless spout, these bloody morons, something that looks *as if* it will pour, that has all the *characteristics* of something *suggestive of* the *act* of pouring, but which in point of fact does not, cannot *pour*, is *incapable of* if not *antithetical to* pouring.

Mr. Peck (to the teacher): Why are you against the war? Why are you for it?

I think it's in my country's best interest.

Well, I don't.

Why?

Mom: Please, no argue!

I'm an English teacher, not a politician or a general, the teacher said, but if I had to give an answer I'd say because it's an ideological war being fought under extremely bad conditions by obsolete means with unspecific goals on behalf of a repressive regime in response to an amorphous threat in a country very far away. Call me a pessimist, but if you ask me the signs don't bode well.

Thanks to attitudes such as yours I too have my doubts.

Please – is Christmas! Who care about war? *I no give a goop!*

I agree, your father said. Let's talk about something else.

This country is on the brink of insurrection.

If it's dissent against the state you're worried about, you seem to be all for it when it comes to swimming pools.

A swimming pool isn't a matter of national security.

But your right to object to it is. You don't want the government building swimming pools, I don't want it fighting a war in Vietnam. You stand for your democratic rights as you see fit. So do I. In that sense we don't disagree.

In that sense you're right, said Mr. Peck.

Pa'al climbed onto the dining room table.

That's my cue, said Mr. Peck, rising, turning to the teacher. Can I offer you a lift home, or are you planning another Polar expedition?

I'll walk, thanks, said the teacher.

WITH MR. PECK gone, you showed the teacher the Building. George went with you. You took a flashlight and used your father's key. The front room was empty and smelled of dust. You passed through a second door into the main part of the laboratory, where the fluorescent lights flickered to life.

Watch out for holes in the floor, you cautioned.

You led the teacher to your father's latest invention, a machine for measuring the thickness of shoe soles. It took up the better part of the main room. You showed him your father's typewriter, his oscilloscope, his basket of oranges, the shelf that sagged under the weight of his notebooks crammed with drawings, notes, and diagrams.

The teacher stepped up to a small crude painting on the wall of the Spanish Steps.

One of your father's?

You nodded.

He writes books, too, said George. Science fiction, philosophy, psychology, etymology. He even wrote a book about grammar.

A polymath.

What's that?

Someone who does many things well.

You showed the teacher the electric motor you'd built.

Interesting. Does it work?

You shook your head.

Peter's inventions only work on paper, said your brother.

BACK AT THE house you heard the sound of water running in the downstairs bathroom as your father flossed his teeth. Your mother washed and put away dishes. George said goodnight and went to bed.

The teacher said:

I should be heading off.

Wait! your mother said. Please – stay a little more long. Have some liqueur. *Una goccietta di Strega.* Peter, go upstair wid you brother.

I'm not tired!

Den go do you omework.

It's Christmas, Mom! I don't have any homework!

Give Peter some omework so we can talk in private.

YOU TOOK THE hint and went downstairs to your new bedroom in what had been the playroom and that you'd adorned with scented candles and blue glass telegraph line insulators, and equipped with a two-burner electric stove to boil water for smoky-tasting tea that you served (to yourself, having no one else to serve it to) in a small pottery mug with no handle. In the middle of the floor you built your own Japanese style table from a slab of unvarnished wood, with cushions around it and a chess set – nice but not as fancy as the teacher's – at its center.

Having made a point of walking loudly down the stairs you waited a few moments before you crept back up them again and sat there, with your ear pressed to the door, imagining your mother and the teacher sitting across from each other in the breakfast nook holding little glasses of yellow liquor. You heard her ask him some questions of which you understood only every third or fourth word, enough to gather that she had concerns. Among other things she had trouble understanding what interest a twenty-four year-old man had in a boy half his age. It wasn't that she did not trust him, so you understood your mother to say.

I'm sure you a good man, she said. Still, I his madder. I need to be sure.

It was the teacher's turn to speak then. His voice was clearer. He told your mother that he would never, ever hurt you or want to see you hurt. Furthermore he said that he cared about you, that you were important to him, very important. He went on to explain that he'd made very few friends in Bethel, that when he wasn't at school or with you he spent most of his time alone, that without you he would have been extremely lonesome, unbearably lonesome.

Honestly, he said. I don't know what I'd do if not for Peter. He's the best if not the only real friend I have around here. If not for him I'd be gone by now. As it stands, I'm not sure how long I'll be staying here. But I will tell you this much: I'd never, ever do anything to hurt him. Ever.

Your mother made the teacher give her his word. He did.

You'd heard enough. You crept back down the stairs and went to bed.

AS A CHILD I SUFFERED TERRIBLY FROM BOREDOM, FROM *the sense that life was hidden away from me somewhere, always a street or a neighborhood or a park or a town removed from wherever I happened to be.*

There are three kinds of children: bored, dull, and curious. The curious are the lucky ones. They'll become scientists, engineers, historians. The dull fair well, too; their paths through life will be relatively smooth and painless, getting along, asking few questions, rarely troubled by existential doubts. The dull make faithful employees and good providers.

Of the three dispositions, boredom is the most troubling. The bored child is both dissatisfied with his environment and unwilling to probe its depths in search of hidden pleasures. Instead of digging into the world, he refutes its surfaces. He craves something "more" but lacks the initiative to obtain it. Like curious children, bored children are inwardly driven, only instead of being benign or beneficent, the forces that drive them are demonic and despotic; they feel tyrannized by boredom. The curious child looks around and wonders how the world works, what is it made of, how did it get here? The bored child looks around at the same world and says, "Where is it? And why am I here and not there?" He doesn't see it as part of himself, something he belongs to that isn't separate and distinct from him.

Having a twin brother didn't help. Rather than solve the problem of boredom, it compounded it, the way a mirror on the wall of a room doubles its size. This may be one reason why I fought so much with George, my twin. I wanted to smash the mirror that doubled my boredom.

It also helps explain my attraction to the new teacher. In him I saw a means of escape from my own sense of boredom, from the limitations of my own existence, a means to redefine myself as my father had redefined himself, and so did the teacher.

* * *

IT GETS LONELY HERE.

The days aren't so bad. I fill them with teaching, swimming, writing. Evenings can be a challenge: exercises in solitude arranged around one-pot meals and disappointing books. Nights are often equally challenging exercises in insomnia.

The town where I live is too small to fuel a decent social life, and so I've taken to inviting my graduate students over regularly to swim off my dock and cook meals together with me. Some may wonder if they're taking advantage of their kindly, middle-aged professor, but I know the opposite to be the case.

It could be worse, I could not have this A-frame on a lake, the dock, the view of water through majestic pines. I live in a beautiful place, everyone says so. Those sunsets across the water – aren't they some sort of victory? Do they not signify, at some level, the approval of – if not a sentient creator – of nature? At such moments, my solitude doesn't seem so bad; I almost forget that my daughter lives a thousand miles away. Otherwise, except when absorbed by my work, I miss Audrey terribly.

I remember our last visit together, her walking over and climbing on my bed with the sun barely risen, saying, "Daddy – it's morning!" She's heavenly, an angel. That all fathers think so of their daughters makes no difference. She is a miraculous creature.

Audrey loves playing this game with me in the morning. I tell her to get up and she says, "No!" Again I command her, and again she disobeys, and so on, until it's time for the Wake-Up Machine, the soft pillow with which I strike her – not really hard, but hard enough to have her ducking under the sheets, giggling. When I stop she says, "Do it again!" and I hit her a few more times with the harmless pillow. "Again,

Daddy, again!" Then I drop the pillow and tickle her until she falls off the bed, and keep tickling her as she squirms in delightful agony across the bedroom floor. At such times being a father is great good fun.

Those are the kinds of things I think about lying in bed alone or sitting on my dock once the sun has set, or after an evening spent with my students, when they've driven home, leaving me to my sunset, a shot of cheap scotch, this pen and this notebook.

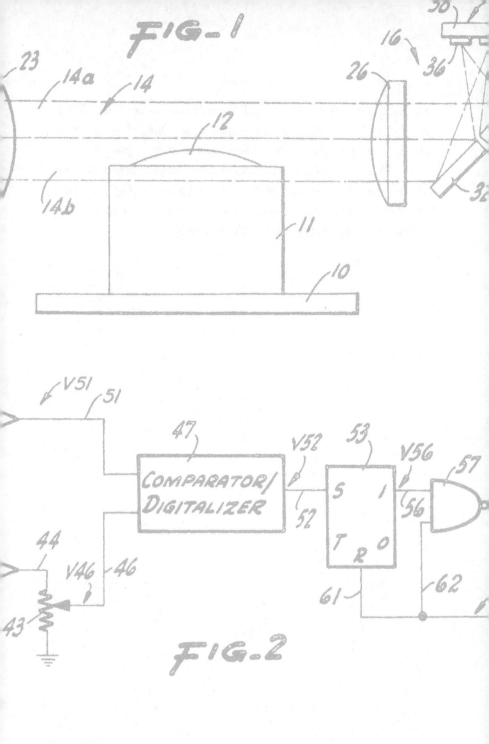

FIG-1

FIG-2

IX.
Self-Actualization
Bethel, Connecticut, 1970

THOUGH YOU SPENT A LOT OF TIME TOGETHER, YOU knew very little about the teacher. He rarely spoke of his family. He kept no mementos in his cottage, no photographs, albums, or objects supplying clues to his past.

He told you that he'd been adopted, that he never knew his real parents. His adoptive mother lived on Lake Lillinonah – or was it Lake Zoar? – in a town less than twenty miles away from Bethel. He had three adoptive siblings, two brothers and a sister, all of them older than he. His oldest brother served as an army first lieutenant in Vietnam. The other brother was a quadriplegic. His name was Frank. In his senior year of high school, he broke his neck while diving into the lake off the top of a steel bridge. Before that, he'd abused the teacher constantly. Now he lived with his mother.

When the teacher was sixteen and had just gotten his learner's permit, he was driving a VW Beetle with Frank, his paralyzed brother, in the passenger seat, when they had an accident. It was a winter afternoon. The roads were icy and your future teacher was arguing with his brother, screaming and crying, when suddenly he lost control of the car. It may have been the ice, the teacher said, or maybe he swerved in anger, or he wanted to have an accident, to kill them both. The car rammed through a guardrail and rolled down an embankment. It rolled ten times before coming to rest on its passenger side a few feet from a frozen pond. The teacher explained how he'd climbed out of the car and stood there, unable to see through the blood, how it had seeped through his fingers as he cupped his shredded face in his hands. Frank survived the accident without a scratch. That was how the teacher got the scar on his face.

That was all you knew about the teacher's past. That and that he'd gone to Oxford on a Rhodes Scholarship before earning his undergraduate degree at Berkeley.

* * *

ABOUT YOUR FATHER'S PAST YOU KNEW ALMOST AS LIT-tle. Whenever you'd ask him questions about his past your father gave brief, grudging answers, or he'd dismiss your questions with a wave of his hand and an *augh!* or some other sound indicative of disinterest, disgust, or displeasure. *What does it matter, Peter? Why should you care?*

Still, every so often a story about your father's past would leak out of him, like the one about the time when his father came home from work one day and, for no obvious reason, slapped him across the face. Your father had been five or six years old. Still, six-ty-five years later he'd remember it. Nor had he ever forgiven his father for it.

This was the only thing your father ever told you about his father or about anyone or anything to do with his family, for that matter. Otherwise it was as if his family had never existed.

There was one other story, though, one your father didn't tell but that you somehow knew anyway, the one about his father, your grandfather, being run over by a streetcar. It came to you spontaneously, like a vision, or you concocted it, but you saw it as clearly in your mind as though it were projected on a screen in a movie theater.

Guido Senigaglia, a severe-looking man with pince-nez and a pointy gray beard, dressed in a three-piece banker's suit adorned with a golden watch fob and a narrow-brimmed black Borsalino, crossing a busy thoroughfare on the way to the bank where he works. He stops to look at his pocket watch, not realizing that he's done so in the middle of the streetcar tracks. By the time he sees the orange streetcar coming it's too late. The vision ends with a scream reverberating through the bustling, cable-crossed streets of Milan.

Like methane gas from a murky, weedy swamp, now and then other bits of your father's past bubbled to the surface. As they broke some of the bubbles whispered names. *Farnsworth. Diamond Ordnance. Arthur Silz. Kit Davidson. Aiken. Fitts. Fivre. Mark I. Treves* ... There were tantalizing clues and bits of evidence. A pair of worn skis, a faded photograph of your father at the helm of a sailboat, a painting on one of the walls of his laboratory of a series of clay busts in varied tones arranged on a piece of furniture, their faces as vacantly enigmatic as Easter Island statues.

You knew he'd been married three times, twice before meeting your mother, yet he spoke as seldom of his other two wives as of the rest of his family – as if they, too, never existed.

You understood, too, that there had been other women in your father's past, women with whom he'd had affairs, though the word *affair* hadn't yet entered your vocabulary. One name in particular was invoked more than any other during your parents' frequent violent arguments, *Be-reh-nee-chay*, the syllables roaring in flames from your mother's mouth like a movie monster's breath.

Yet you never got the feeling that your father was keeping secrets from you. It was more like he didn't care, like he couldn't be bothered, as though his past didn't exist for him, like he'd forgotten about it the same way he would always forget about little things that didn't matter enough to him, like zipping his fly.

YOUR FATHER DIDN'T believe in God. He was an atheist – a word you learned long before you would learn the words *nuance* or *empathy*, and longer still before you'd come into contact with words like metaphysics or transcendence.

At the corner of Wooster Street and Almar Drive, where you and George waited for the school bus in the morning, Bobby Mullin, who went to Saint Mary's, used to punch you in the face for not believing in God. He'd walk up to you, shove his face into yours, and say, *Do you believe in God?* When you said no he'd punch you. Bobby had pimples and red hair and wore the Catholic school's official green plaid tie over a starched white Oxford cloth shirt. How he knew you didn't believe in God you had no idea. You wondered if maybe there was a Master List of Atheists somewhere and, if so, who was in charge of it. For sure your father's name was close to the top.

Though your father was an electronics engineer and inventor, his wasn't the calm, rational, detached atheism of a scientist. The engine of his disbelief ran hot and would boil over from time to time. He reserved a special loathing for televangelists. However fleeting, the appearance of a flashy-toothed, pompadoured preacher on television sufficed to deliver him through a profusion of profanities to apoplexy's door.

Papa didn't believe in belief, such was the magnitude of his skepticism. The words belief and faith made him cringe. *What does it mean – to "have faith"? What imbecility! When people say they "believe" in something or other, what do they mean, other than that they've stopped thinking? What's so bloody wonderful about that?*

No, your father wasn't built for belief. Or faith or patriotism or pride. Logical creature that he was, he could no more bring himself to feel such things than he could salute the flag, throw a football, or drop to his knees and pray to an Almighty Creator.

Your father's lack of pride, faith, and devotion extended to his children. Blood may have been thicker than water, but so what? What did that have to do with anything?

From your father you'd inherit your own atheism, though you'd resist calling yourself an atheist, the word sounded so hostile, so harsh, as if you were God's sworn enemy rather than someone who didn't – couldn't – believe in him.

THERE WAS ONE more clue to your father's past – not a clue, really, but a question, namely why did he treat his mother, your grandmother, Nonnie, so badly, calling her stronzo and other names whenever she dared to venture forth from the little corner room where she lived like an in-house prisoner, reading *Reader's*

Digest, watching Arthur Godfrey, listening to her radio – a brown Bakelite job with a round dial?

On her way to the bathroom – the downstairs bathroom with the plum-colored fixtures – he'd intercept her, cutting her off, offering admittance begrudgingly or refusing it outright. The bathroom was ever an item of contention between them. It belonged to the house, but it was Papa's bathroom, where he flossed his teeth and kept his unguents and implements and medications, his safety razor, his Sominex, his Senokot, his Desinex. He kept his bathrobe there, too, the battered terrycloth one, with its odor of musk and dander, that special smell that whispered *Papa* to you when you'd take a whiff or when you'd wear the robe, enshrouding yourself in your father's essence.

STRONZO! Papa would bellow at his mother on her way to the bathroom with her cane.[5] She'd stop and stand there, frozen, clutching her cane, bewildered, pupils dilating, her eyes searching those of her only child for forgiveness, for a reprieve, for mercy, asking *What have I done?* getting no answer, for by then her son would already be red-faced with laughter, his titters conveying him the rest of the way to his purple fortress, to resound – together with the sound of the door slamming – off its plum-colored tiles.

What terrible thing had his mother – your grandmother – done to him?

One anecdote provided a partial explanation. Like the one about his father slapping him it was the only story your father ever told you about his mother.

He was nine or ten years old. His father had just recently died. In preparation for a move to a much smaller apartment, his mother was sorting through their belongings, deciding what items to keep and which to throw away. She kept her collection of Japanese fans and threw out your father's favorite toy: a locomotive that ran on live steam, with a real boiler and pistons of shiny brass. She threw

---

5   The word literally means "large turd," but is used more generally to characterize a reprehensible human being.

it into the rubbish bin. By the time your future father found out, the *basurero* – the garbage man – had come and gone.

For that, apparently, your father never forgave his mother.

Still there had to be more to this otherwise gentle man of sixty abusing his mother, the same mother he'd kept close to him for so many years, across an ocean and through three marriages, to explain why he did so so constantly, so viciously, with such relish.

You might have asked him but you didn't, knowing he'd have shrugged and waved his hand and said *aughh* in that way of his, as if the question were beneath contempt, as if only an imbecile would ask such a stupid question.

* * *

FROM *THE THEORY OF HUMAN MOTIVATION*, A BOOK THE teacher let you borrow, you learned that humans attain their ultimate potential through a process called "self-actualization," which, to be achieved, requires that lower and more basic needs be fulfilled. The book's author, Abraham Maslow, organized his scale of needs into a pyramid, with basic needs at the bottom and self-actualization at the pinnacle.

The concept of self-actualization engrossed you. You were enchanted by the vision of an army of human beings mounting ladders of needs, from the elementary (food, water) through the prosaic (safety, shelter, stability) through more refined yet still fundamental needs (comfort, love, sensual gratification, a sense of belonging), to the summit where they became "actualized." They realized their true potentials as men and women capable of the highest forms of expression, kindness, resourcefulness, and generosity.

What about all the people who spend their whole lives just trying to eat, struggling for survival? you asked the teacher. Does that mean they'll never self-actualize?

According to Maslow it does, the teacher said.

It doesn't seem fair.

Who says it is?

You were in the teacher's cottage, sitting at the Japanese-style table. Stravinsky's *Firebird* played on the record player. You'd drunk tea and played two games of chess and wrestled. You said:

I wonder where I am on Maslow's pyramid.

Let's find out, said the teacher. I assume your physiological needs have been met?

I've got a bed to sleep in. And I'm not starving.

Glad to hear it. Do you feel safe?

Pretty much.

What about your social needs? Would you say you're loved?

I guess so.

Bullshit. You know damned well you are. What about your sense of belonging? Do you feel accepted by society at large?

Sure. Most of the time.

How's your self-esteem?

You shrugged. It's not bad.

The teacher pursed his lips and nodded.

Sounds to me like you're ready to self-actualize, he said.

ON MY LAST TRIP NORTH TO VISIT HER, I TOOK AUDREY *to Mystic Seaport. It was one of those rare perfect days life dishes up every few years. It was supposed to rain, but for once I cast aside my skepticism and decided to go anyway. The weather turned out to be more than fine: a few clouds, otherwise cool and very dry. The seaport wasn't crowded; at times it felt as if we had the place to ourselves. We began with a short ride on a steamboat – a lovely two-decker with the sweetest little engine, this guileless contraption with pistons that made a gentle* pssst-pssst *sound as they reciprocated and the young engineer doubled as the stoker. The captain let Audrey take the helm and steer the boat in its circular course around the harbor. Afterward we visited the cooper, who let Audrey roll one of her barrels, and the blacksmith, who fashioned an iron heart for her in her forge. The white-hot heart sizzled when dipped in a basin of cool water. Then Daddy rented a vintage rowboat and rowed his sweetheart around the harbor. A pause for beverages at the Spouter Inn (Daddy: pale bitter ale, Audrey: lemonade) followed by an exhibit on the refurbishing of the whale ship Charles W. Morgan and a ride on an antique electric launch. I'd hoped for us to sail, but when we got to the rental office the last sailboat had departed.*

Only as we were driving home on the Merritt Parkway did it start to rain. On the last leg up Route 7 the skies cleared. The sun broke through the clouds at just the right angle, forming an enormous rainbow, the first live specimen my daughter had seen. Fortuitously, it followed us the rest of the way home. I thought to myself: that rainbow is something she will remember. Its colors will burn themselves into her brain. Egocentrically, I thought from now on whenever she sees a rainbow Audrey will remember this trip and think of her daddy.

One of the chief purposes of life: to supply the illusion of paradise to children.

A week after I returned to Georgia, Audrey's mother sent me a photo of her latest watercolor masterpiece. Title: The Rainbow.

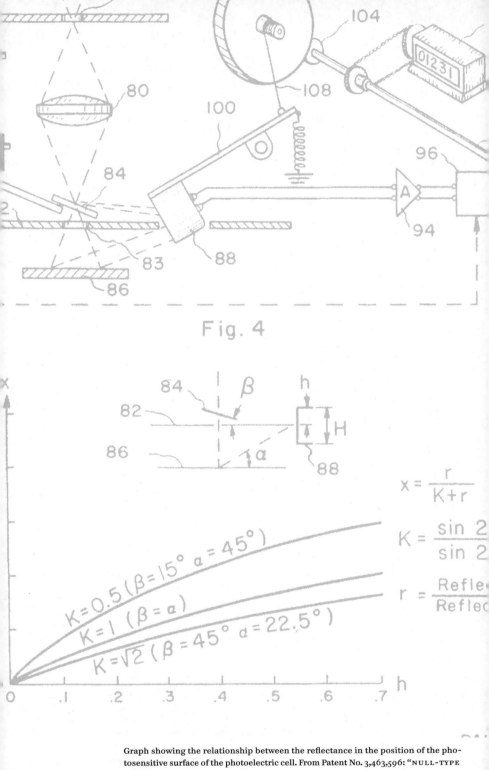

Fig. 4

$$x = \frac{r}{K+r}$$

$$K = \frac{\sin 2}{\sin 2}$$

$$r = \frac{Refle}{Refle}$$

K=0.5 (β=15° α=45°)

K=1 (β=α)

K=√2 (β=45° α=22.5°)

Graph showing the relationship between the reflectance in the position of the photosensitive surface of the photoelectric cell. From Patent No. 3,463,596: "NULL-TYPE COMPARISON REFLECTOMETER WHEREIN NULLING IS ACCOMPLISHED BY MOVING THE LIGHT DETECTOR."

X.
The Man in the Wheelchair
Bethel, Connecticut, 1970

CERTAIN MEMORIES REPLAY THEMSELVES WITH THE sounds and colors all drained out of them, like a worn-out old silent movie, covered with spots and scratches that look like a snowstorm. You'll wonder if the movie was real or if you invented it.

One afternoon in February, a few days before your fourteenth birthday, you walked to the teacher's cottage. You carried a paperback copy of *Man and His Symbols,* a collection of essays on Jungian thought that the teacher had urged upon you and that you'd read most of and were eager to discuss with him. You were especially eager to discuss the idea of the "collective unconscious," Jung's belief in the existence of a sort of communal warehouse wherein impersonal human experiences were collected and universally shared – a notion that, if he didn't find it entirely reprehensible, your hyper-rational father would nevertheless have rejected.

Which may have been why you embraced it.

When you got there, you found a white van parked in front of the cottage, not an ordinary van, but one with a ramp coming out of the sliding side door and the words TIP-TOP AMBULETTE painted backward across the back, so what it really said was ETTELUBMA POT-PIT. No sooner did you see it parked there than you felt your gut muscles drop and your heart started racing. The teacher has had a heart attack, you said to yourself. He's had a heart attack and died and you would never see him again. You'd never play chess or drink smoky tea or collect old bottles or walk along the train tracks in search of glass insulators. Everything would go back to being just the way it was before, as if you and the teacher had never met, like it was all just a dream.

Those were your thoughts as you gazed at the back doors of the white van through the flakes of what was forecast to be the first major snowstorm of the New Year.

Please God no, you prayed. *Please don't let the teacher be dead. Don't even let him be hurt or sick.* You reminded yourself then that you didn't believe in god, so instead you prayed to the collective unconscious.

You stepped up to the blue door and were about to knock when you heard a voice yelling inside. It didn't sound like the teacher, but then you had never heard the teacher yelling before, you'd never heard him raise his voice. The screaming continued. There were two voices then: a raspy, deep, throaty growl – a voice so gravelly you could have mixed concrete with it – and a calm, subdued, familiar voice that you recognized as the teacher's. You could have pressed your ear to the door and heard more, but you decided not to. You'd already heard more than you wanted to. You wished you hadn't gone to the teacher's cottage at all that day.

You'd turned and were starting back to the road when suddenly you heard the blue door open (in cold weather it tended to stick to the jamb so when opened it made an obscene sound). You turned to see a man in a wheelchair, a scary-looking man with something wrong with one side of his face, being pushed by the ambulance attendant, a dark-skinned man in a white suit. As they neared the van you got a clearer look at the face of the man in the wheelchair. Though one side looked normal the other was a pink-orange color that looked almost fluorescent, like those street signs warning of detours and lane closures. The skin on that side was stretched tightly like a Halloween mask. The wheelchair bound man's hair had something wrong with it, too. Black and stiff, it looked like a dead crow squatting on his head.

The man in the wheelchair was smoking. That seemed wrong, too. Someone in a wheelchair had enough problems, you thought. While waiting for him to finish smoking, the attendant, who was tall and thin, leaned against the van. Finished, the man in the wheelchair tossed the butt onto the rear tire of the van.

By then the snow was falling faster, the flurries blowing in all directions. Through them you saw the attendant help the man in the wheelchair onto the ramp. Then, at the back of the van, the attendant pressed a button or pulled a lever. The ramp lifted up and drew itself in, like a tongue, into the van's gaping mouth. The attendant returned to the side of the van, said something to the man in the wheelchair, and closed the van's side door before climbing into the driver's seat. He sat there for some time with the engine running and puffs of smoke exhaling from the tailpipe.

Then he backed the ambulance out into the street and drove away.

Everything was quiet for a while then in the way things get suddenly quiet after a disaster. You stood there in the silence trying to decide whether or not to knock on the carriage house door. You were about to do so when you heard a sound coming from inside. The teacher was crying. There was no doubt about it. Through the blue door you heard breathless sobs. You stood there listening, wondering what to feel.

The crying stopped.

You turned and walked away, home through the snowflakes without stopping, past the gas station and the railroad tracks and the library and Mullaney's store, determined to forget this experience, to pretend that it never happened. But you wouldn't forget.

IF I MIX A LITTLE FICTION WITH MY NONFICTION, A LITTLE *lie with the truth, it's by way of making the truth even truer. Think of Ellison's invisible man adding his single drop of black to an enormous vat of white paint to make it "whiter." The truth works in this paradoxical way, I think, since to give it context, to put it into perspective, the truth's "truthfulness" demands a touch of dishonesty, just as the most intense pleasure demands a measure of pain or as the brightness of a rose in landscape painting depends upon the relative dullness of the surrounding plants and flowers. You can't have the truth without lies. Or you can – it may be there – but you won't see it, it won't stand out. I think what I'm saying here is that lies brighten up the truth. The key is to blend them – those drops of black paint – thoroughly so they're invisible to the naked eye.*

* * *

THE ELOQUENCE AND POETRY OF PAPA'S PATENT APPLICATIONS *("The secondary flux which links with the line winding is seen to consist also of two components. Of these one has the line frequency ωL, the other the frequency $\omega L - 4\omega R$."), how they manage, or try very hard, to achieve a scrupulous objectivity, something that (as every writer knows) is hard if not impossible (see Robbe-Grillet).*

Compare and contrast your father's patents with the memoir you're writing and which the reader is reading: how different they are as "performances." Though not all the inventions they describe were successful, however successful they were, as pieces of writing, as works of postmodern art or irony (something like the "postmodern" motor you built in the Building's back room), they're impressive and even sublime in their eloquence. And this memoir? What it can't claim in objectivity or accuracy or even integrity – does is make up for in "art"?

> This reconstructive nature of memory can make it unreliable. The information from which an autobiographical memory is constructed may be more or less accurately stored, but it needs to be integrated according to the demands of the present moment, and errors and distortions can creep in at every stage. The end result may be vivid and convincing, but vividness does not guarantee accuracy. A coherent story about the past can sometimes only be won at the expense of the memory's correspondence to reality. Our memories of childhood, in particular, can be highly unreliable. Thinking differently about memory requires us to think differently about some of the "truths" that are closest to the core of our selves.
>
> CHARLES FERNYHOUGH, *Pieces of Light*

> I refuse to regard remembrance the way the rest of you usually do, as a very clumsy form of self-expression. When something great, serious, beautiful happens to us, there's no need to pursue it afterward in memory; rather this event must from the outset merge with our innermost being, meld with it, shape within us a new and better "I," and live inside us eternally, co-creating ourselves into the future.
>
> GOETHE, in a letter to pianist Maria Szymanowska

> When I use my memory, I ask it to produce whatever it is that I wish to remember.
>
> AUGUSTINE, *Confessions*

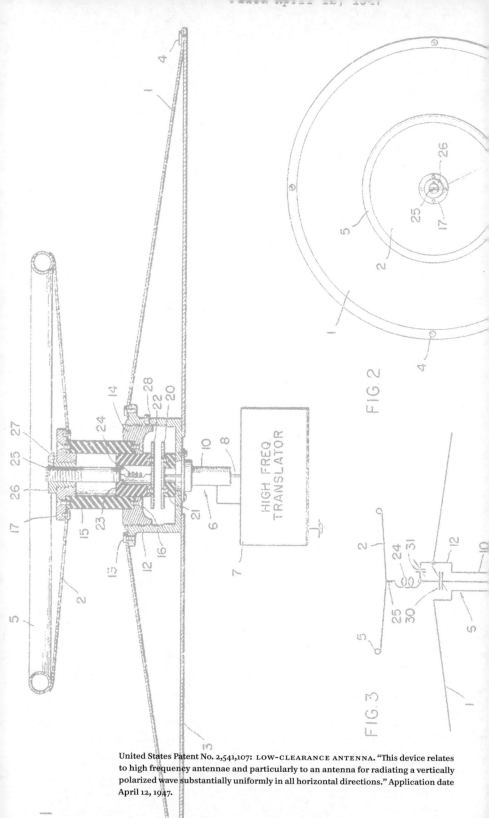

United States Patent No. 2,541,107: LOW-CLEARANCE ANTENNA. "This device relates to high frequency antennae and particularly to an antenna for radiating a vertically polarized wave substantially uniformly in all horizontal directions." Application date April 12, 1947.

XI.
Everything You've Learned is Wrong
Bethel, Connecticut, 1970–1971

YOU ADMIRED THE TEACHER'S INTENSITY, HIS IDEALISM, the relentlessness of his standards, his intolerance of small, narrow minds, of pettiness and mediocrity.

Mediocre: it was a word the teacher used constantly. Most adults – the same mass of men that Henry David Thoreau characterized as "leading lives of quiet desperation" – were mediocre. They accumulated and spent money. They ate and slept. They fornicated and reproduced and carried out other biological, social, and economic imperatives while watching too much television. They lived their lives less in accordance with their principles or in response to their own unique perceptions than in timorous obeisance to conformity and authority. They were ignorant, insular, shallow, backwards, and provincial. They indulged in petty discourses and rivalries. They lacked imagination and creativity. They were to be pitied and feared: mostly feared, since they were dangerous.

What people don't understand they tend to hold suspect and resent, the teacher said to you one day as you sat with him in his cottage. And the sad truth is most people understand very little. Why do you think there's so much persecution in the world? Jews persecuted by Christians, Catholics by Protestants, Buddhists by Hindus, Muslims by Buddhists, blacks, Latinos, and Asians by whites.... It comes down to the same thing: people fearing those not of their ilk, who don't think or act as they do. What they really fear is love, is their own innate sense of compassion. They fear it as a weakness.

You see it right here in this town, the teacher went on to say, all around you, on a much smaller scale. You've experienced it yourself, I'm sure.

You nodded, recalling Bobby Mullin punching you at the bus stop.

IT WAS MAINLY through the teacher that you first came to realize the frailties and fallibility of adults. The more he frowned on them in your presence, the more he called them "mediocre," the more you took for granted that you yourself would never be "mediocre," that you would be – in fact you already were – above average: special.

This sense of superiority didn't come without a price. To earn it you worked hard. The teacher's standards were high not just for himself but for you and all his students, especially those in his fifth-period class. His homework assignments were challenging and copious. You had to read a book every two weeks, and write one paper, and sometimes more than one. On top of that, each of you had to produce one long paper for the term, at least fifty pages long and typed. All this and your creative projects, stories, poems, songs, short plays, and films. To these projects you were encouraged – required – to bring not only the ability to read and write, but as many skills as possible: drawing, painting, music, sculpture – even, when appropriate, science, mechanics, and magic.

Halfway through the spring semester, at the teacher's urging and under his supervision, you and your fifth-period classmates launched *The Hatted Tattler*, Bethel Middle School's first ever underground newspaper. It featured two op-ed pieces, one protesting the Vietnam War, the other against the school's long-standing injunction against wearing hats in the hallways.

No sooner was the underground newspaper distributed early one Wednesday morning than the administration snatched it – its pages still warm and reeking from the spirit duplicator – out of the grips of curious students, and marched its distributors to the office of the principal, who doled out suspensions to each of them.

It wasn't long before, red-faced and indignant, the teacher appeared. With the principal, the vice principal, and himself behind it, the principal's door closed. It remained closed for the next half hour or so, after which the teacher emerged. Without a word, he guided his flock back to their respective classrooms.

That afternoon in the G.P. (general purpose) room, the student body gathered for a special assembly. With you and your fifth-period classmates seated in the very first row, on behalf of the entire school administration, the principle apologized for having "inadvertently interfered" with your First-Amendment right to free speech.

SUCH VICTORIES WEREN'T without controversy. They put many noses out of joint.

Meanwhile, rumors about the teacher spread and flourished. He was a communist, an agitator, a radical spreading lies, propaganda, and dissent, corrupting the town's impressionable youth. His methods were not merely experimental, they were subversive. *Desks in a circle! Underground newspapers!* When not having orgies with them, he did heroin, LSD, and other drugs with his pupils.

You had to laugh, you and your brother and others in the teacher's special class, the rumors were so outrageous and unfounded. Even the teacher found them laughable, to a point, until the rumors singled you out for slander.

Have you heard what they're saying about us? the teacher asked you one afternoon in his cottage a few days after your fourteenth birthday.

No, you answered (though of course you knew perfectly well).

When the teacher repeated the worst of the rumors, you smiled.

You find it amusing?

Sure. Don't you?

No, said the teacher. And neither should you. I don't see anything amusing about it.

Let them say whatever they want. Why should we care?

I wish it were that simple, the teacher said, frowning.

Why should we care what a bunch of stupid, gossiping, nar-row-minded mediocre assholes think? ("Narrow-minded" was another term the teacher had taught you, along with "mediocre," "tunnel-visioned," and "self-satisfied.") Hell, we shouldn't even be talking about them. We shouldn't dignify them with this conversation.

I'm afraid we need to talk about it, Peter.

Since when? Since when do other people's opinions matter that much to you?

Since they may end up hurting you.

Fuck them. They can go to hell!

You were sitting at the teacher's Japanese-style table. A fire belched and roared in the stove. The teapot sat cold in its cozy on the table alongside your two drained cups. On the chessboard the chess pieces were arrayed in their starting positions.

You don't have to worry about me, you said, moving a white pawn. I can look after myself.

You sound awfully sure about that, said the teacher, mov-ing his own pawn.

It was a question. You moved a second pawn. The teacher did likewise.

I know who I am, you said. I don't need anyone else to tell me.

You advanced one of your two bishops.

The teacher waited a moment before speaking. Then, having moved a knight, quietly, he said:

How can you know who you are? You're still a work in process.

You said nothing. You moved another pawn.

You've only just turned fourteen. In ways, you're mature. In other ways, you're still growing up. Don't be offended, Peter. Hear me out. The point is you're still very young; you have a lot to learn. You've barely encountered reality. You haven't suffered yet, not yet, not in the ways that adults suffer. You've experienced some joys and pleasures, but you still haven't known the half of either.

You said nothing. You moved a rook.

I'm not criticizing you, Peter, just stating a few facts. When you leave here later on today you'll go home to your parents, who feed you and keep a roof over your head and see to it that your lower needs – the ones at the bottom of Maslow's pyramid – are met. Your folks also fulfill your higher needs by caring about you in other ways.

The teacher conveyed his queen to the other end of the board, where it challenged your bishop. You slid a pawn into its path.

You don't know what it's like to be completely on your own, the teacher said, with all the forces of the world bearing down on you, forces that can twist and corrupt you in all kinds of ways. They'll go after your humanity, Peter. They'll attack it the way white blood cells attack bacteria. You'll have to fight them. I hope you'll turn out to be one of the lucky ones, that you'll end up being as strong in the future as you think you are now. I really hope so.

As you moved your own knight you felt tears tugging at the corners of your eyes.

But it'll be a while before we know that, won't it? Until then, I have to take some responsibility for your future, Peter. Not just as your teacher, but as a friend. Which is why – he paused – I think we should start seeing a little less of each other.

You felt a tightness in the far back of your throat as more tears tugged at your eyes. You did your best to hide these things, along with the other signs of distress, but it was like hiding a highway billboard.

Don't take it so hard, the teacher said, reaching his hand over to grasp yours. We'll get through this. You'll see. It won't be so bad. You'll come here with George and your other friends. Come with them as often as you like. And we can still get together otherwise, just not quite so often. Okay?

You nodded. But you knew it wouldn't be the same. For a while you'd existed in a special realm all your own, enjoying its privileges, partaking in its rites and rituals, relishing and sheltering the mysteries and sacred orders of its reign. Now that kingdom – one small enough to fit into a former carriage house, its command post an unvarnished slab of tea-soaked wood – had run its course, and with it your role as young prince and counselor to the emperor.

The teacher changed the subject then, announcing that he

had a birthday present for you: a travelling chess set, one much smaller but nearly as beautiful as his, with squares of rosewood and holly and closing lid flaps.

* * *

ENGLISH NIGHT TOOK PLACE THE THIRD WEEK OF FEB-ruary. It was held in the G.P. Room and open to the general public. There would be readings of poems, short stories, and short plays, as well as screenings of short films and displays of journals, term papers, and other creations of the students in the teacher's fifth-period English class.

The crowning event would be the presentation of the English Award for best term paper. Yours was titled "Pollution and its Effects on the Environment." You'd spent a hundred hours on it, typing away on a teal Olivetti that your parents had given you for Christmas. Days before the award ceremony, the teacher took you aside and warned you that, though your term paper was indeed the best, you wouldn't win the award.

It wouldn't look right, the teacher told you. It's not exactly a secret that you and I are friends. People will assume I'm playing favorites. You do understand, right?

And though you had understood, when the time came for the award announcement, in the gloom backstage, in that realm of curtains, ropes, battens, sandbags, and dimmer boards (all stained blood-red by workers' lights), it tortured you to know that Vivian – whose term paper was about Sylvia Plath ("Sylvia: The Life and Death of a Poet") – would win, despite the fact that not only was her paper shorter than yours by eleven pages, its subject had been dimwitted enough to stick her head in an oven.

As the teacher reeled off the names of the finalists you stood there, choking back your tears, hearing the words "winner" and "Vivian" paired over and over again, so often and loudly that when it came you weren't sure you heard the real announcement correctly. Then you heard it again, unmistakably clear this time.

You'd won the English Night Award for Best Term Paper.

As he handed you the citation, the teacher whispered: *Fuck 'em.*

A WEEK LATER, that's when you learned that the teacher was leaving.

It was a Saturday after another blizzard. Everything was covered in snow. You and the teacher walked to a nearby playground, one with three baseball diamonds. At the remotest and least used of them, you wiped the snow off the bleachers and sat. High over your heads, on top of the rusty backstop, a pair of crows cawed extravagantly, reminding you of the fight your parents had the evening before, one that ended with your mother scrawling with a black china marker on the living room walls that she had just painted an ugly purple a week earlier. Having agreed to visit him that morning, you left the house early, trudging through drifts of unplowed snow, arriving at the teacher's carriage house with a runny nose and frozen toes. As more snow fell you knocked on the blue door and waited. You knocked again.

The teacher said he'd be there. He promised.

You knocked again. You stomped the soles of the black cowboy boots that you'd impulsively (and foolishly) worn and exhaled into your cupped hands to warm them (in your eagerness you'd forgotten your gloves, too).

On the ground near the doormat on which you'd been stomping you noticed a bent rusty nail. You picked it up. Before you knew it, you were carving the words THANKS FOR KEEPING A PROMISE into the door's blue paint. You carved each letter slowly, carefully. Then you sat down on the icy doormat with your back to the door.

A few minutes later the teacher arrived holding a grocery bag under each arm.

Nice. I'm sure my landlord will be pleased.

I'll pay for it, you said.

The teacher shook his head.

I mean it, you said.

I'm sure you do. In fact I intend to hold you to it.

So how come you're shaking your head?

The teacher smiled. Dear Peter. So easily hurt, so easily hurting others.

THE TEACHER INVITED you in. By then you were freezing. Come, he said, sit by the stove. Not too close, he said. It's not healthy to heat up too suddenly from the cold. I assume you'd like some tea?

After you'd had a cup of tea and warmed up, that's when the teacher suggested a walk to the playground. He had something important he needed to tell you. It was like going to the doctor for a vaccination shot. You know the needle's coming, but when it comes somehow it's still a shock. It still hurts.

Meanwhile the two crows kept cawing – so loudly you couldn't hear yourself think, you couldn't hear a thing. More snow fell. The Catholic Church steeple rose high above the naked treetops. The sky was an inverted gray ocean.

They've put us in a box, the teacher was saying. That's what people do with things they can't understand. They find boxes to put them in and stick labels on them. Whether the labels fit or not doesn't matter.

Where do you plan to go?

I'm not sure. I'll probably travel for a while. I've never been to the Far East. Japan. India. I'll start there, maybe.

When do you plan to leave?

Soon as possible. Frankly – and this is no reflection on you or our friendship, you understand – but I can't bear to be here much longer. I've come to detest this miserable backwater and everything it stands for. Fucking narrow-minded people. They and people like them ruin everything. Give them paradise and they turn it into a shithole. What they can't join or enjoy they destroy or try their best to. Fuck them! If I leave tomorrow it won't be a day too soon. I've already tendered my resignation. Anyway, for your sake it's probably better for me to leave sooner rather than later.

The two crows stopped cawing.

You thought for a moment before you said:

What if I went with you?

The teacher smiled.

I'm not kidding. I've never been to Japan.

I doubt your parents would approve.

That's their problem.

Come on, Peter.

What the hell do I need to stay here for?

You're fourteen.

So what? What does my age have to do with it?

It has everything to do with it.

Besides, after you're gone, I'll still be stuck in that box.

There won't be any box. Not after I'm gone.

How do you know?

I know.

It's not fair, you said.

We'll still be friends. I give you my word on that. I'll write to
you. And as soon as we can we'll see each other again. You'll see. It
won't be so bad. Anyway it's the best solution I can offer.

It isn't fair, you said.

Peter, please –

It isn't, dammit!

Don't be childish.

You stood up and shouted at the two crows:

It isn't fair! It isn't fair! It isn't fucking fair!

The crows flew off.

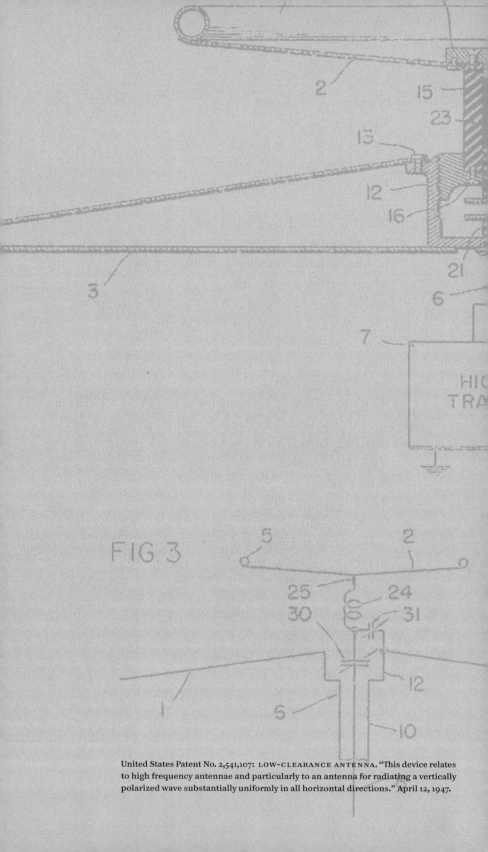

FIG. 3

United States Patent No. 2,541,107: LOW-CLEARANCE ANTENNA. "This device relates to high frequency antennae and particularly to an antenna for radiating a vertically polarized wave substantially uniformly in all horizontal directions." April 12, 1947.

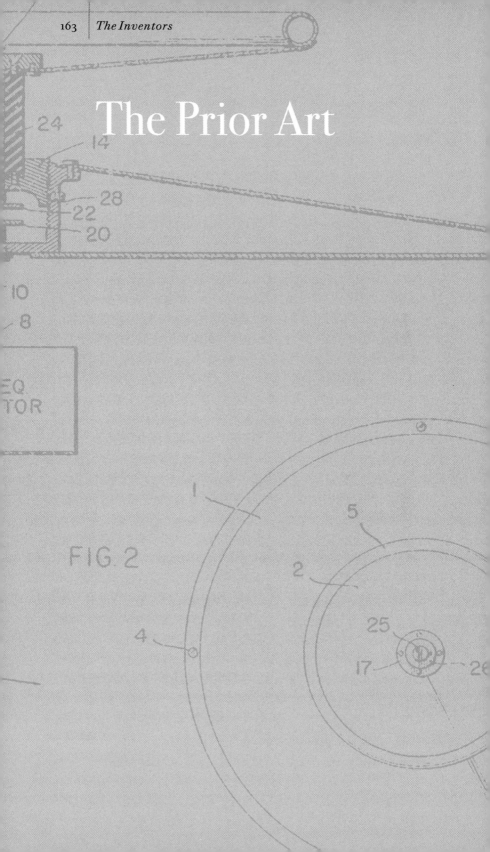

The Prior Art

There is only one problem in the world. How does one burst the pupa and metamorphose into a butterfly?

THOMAS MANN

AN INDIAN BOY APPROACHES HIS GURU, WHO SITS IN A *forest examining a small object in his hand. Asked what the object is, the guru answers:*

It's called a chrysalis and holds an incipient butterfly. In time it will split apart and the butterfly will burst forth on beautiful wings.

The boy asks the guru if he may have it.

Yes, says the guru, under one condition: you must promise that when the butterfly beats its wings against the chrysalis to make it split open, you will resist helping it. You must let the butterfly emerge on its own.

Having made his assurances, the boy takes the chrysalis home, where he watches it, waiting for it to split open. After a few hours, sure enough the chrysalis begins to quiver. The boy sees the half-formed butterfly beating its wings against it, frantically trying to escape. At last the boy can't resist any longer. He breaks open the chrysalis. The butterfly staggers out, falls to the ground, and dies.

Carrying the dead butterfly, with tears in his eyes the boy returns to his guru.

You broke your promise, didn't you? the guru says.

The boy nods. The guru explains:

By beating its wings against the chrysalis the latent butterfly strengthens its muscles, making it possible for him to fly. By helping it as you did you doomed it.

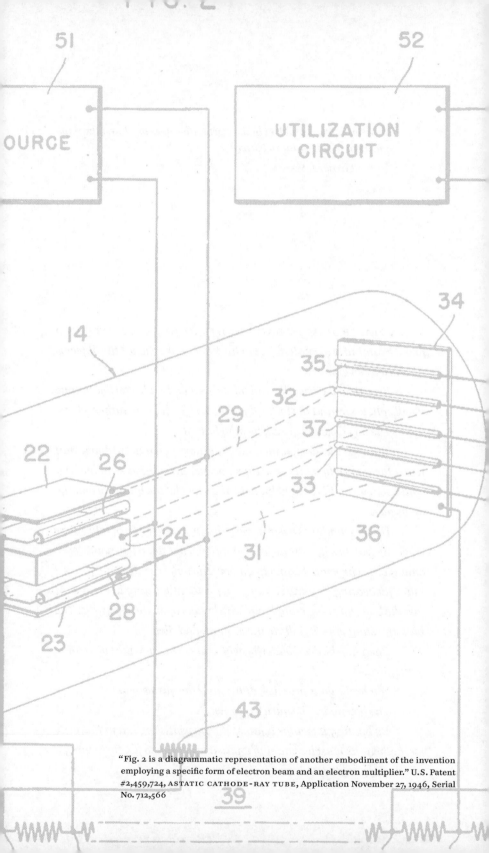

FIG. 2

51

52

OURCE

UTILIZATION
CIRCUIT

14

35

32

34

29

37

22

26

33

24

31

36

28

23

43

39

"Fig. 2 is a diagrammatic representation of another embodiment of the invention employing a specific form of electron beam and an electron multiplier." U.S. Patent #2,459,724, ASTATIC CATHODE-RAY TUBE, Application November 27, 1946, Serial No. 712,566

XII.
If Ever I Would Leave You
Bethel, Connecticut, 1971–1975

THE SUMMER AFTER THE TEACHER LEFT, YOU HELPED your father with one of his inventions. It had been commissioned by the famous dungaree manufacturer Levi Strauss & Co. to measure the number of flaws per inch in bolts of denim fabric. The four-foot wide bolts were fed on a conveyor of chains and rollers through a bed of solar cells that responded electronically to shifts in color, thickness, and light too subtle for human eyes to detect.

Like the Shoe Sole Machine, this was one of your father's bigger and more ambitious inventions. It took up the entire vestibule – the same vestibule that once housed a five-foot long black snake. According to U.S. Patent Number 3,841,761, the machine's official designation was "Apparatus for Detecting Faults in Denim Fabric," but you and your father both called it the "The Blue Jean Machine."

You painted aluminum and sheet metal panels with steel blue and center-punched or scored them for the drill press, the band saw, the bending machine. You drilled, filed, sanded, screwed, bolted, and soldered. Together you and your father watched the Blue Jean Machine grow into a staunch mechanical dinosaur, a stegosaurus of metal and circuitry squatting there in the vestibule, waiting to be fed its bolts of rugged blue denim.

When neighborhood kids came by for a visit you'd point to it and say, Here's what my father and I have been working on lately, as if you'd had a hand not only in executing but in conceiving the contraption.

Working alongside him in his decrepit laboratory that summer, you never felt closer to your inventor papa. When he showed you how to work the drill press or the band saw, you felt the warm roughness of his hand guiding yours. The Building's smells (of orange peels, scorched metal, and solder flux) became your smells; its sounds (of radio static, buzzing fluorescent tubes, and your father's curses and farts) became your sounds. The same metal-filing enriched blood ran through your two sets of veins, to where you almost believed that, catching a glimpse of yourself in a mirror, you'd see not your own face but your father's, with its sloped forehead, its strands of gray hair, its curious large deep-set eyes, its blissfully stretched smile.

A MONTH PASSED with no word from the teacher. Then two, three, six months. ... A year. You wondered if you'd ever hear from him again. Every day that passed without a letter from the teacher was a blow that left you bruised inside. You tried not to think about it. Another part of you, a deeper stronger part that didn't bruise as easily, was sure not only that you'd get a letter but that you'd see him again. It was just a matter of time.

One summer Sunday, as you were fixing the chain on your bicycle, a rusting green convertible Karmann Ghia came up the steep driveway. You stood there watching as a man stepped out of the car.

At first you didn't recognize the teacher. He'd grown a long beard and wore a plaid shirt. He'd lost weight. When you hugged him you could feel the teacher's ribcage.

You said:

I was starting to think I'd never see you again.

Were you?

Where have you been?

That's a long story.

You could have at least written me, you know.

You're right, Peter: I could have.

Why didn't you?

The teacher smiled in that way of his that had the answers but refused, at least for the time being, to share them.

Are your folks around?

Sure. Mom's inside. My father's in his lab. Did you want to see them?

I want to see you. Is there someplace we can go?

IN THE TEACHER'S Karmann Ghia you rode to Huntington State Park. The park was named for Collis Potter Huntington, the railroad robber baron whose summer estate it had once been, and whose daughter Anna, the sculptress, also lived and worked there. On the way, the teacher told you about the project he'd undertaken in Boston, where he had settled following his travels, a special high school program he had designed for bright, underprivileged people, mostly young men from Roxbury and other blighted Boston neighborhoods. He explained how – before moving to Boston – he'd lived for a while in Maine, first in Portland and then in Bangor, where he met a woman, a painter named Eleanor, with whom he had been romantically involved.

I was all set to marry her, he told you as the Karmann Ghia zipped down a series of winding, leafy roads. I proposed and she accepted. Then the Boston job came up.

So what happened?

We broke the engagement. We couldn't work things out. Eleanor didn't want to leave Maine, and I didn't want to give up the chance to do something more important than anything I'd ever done in my life. It's not every day you get the chance to set up a small alternative high school in the ghetto of a major city. I begged her to come with me, but I knew it was hopeless. We both knew it. Having dedicated your whole life to painting trees, you don't pick up and move to Dorchester, Massachusetts. So we broke it off. It really blew my circuits. I've never been more depressed. I felt like killing myself.

I'm glad you didn't.

So am I.

The car's roof was open; the wind blew the teacher's hair and yours.

What about you? Have you been seeing anyone?

You considered filling the teacher in on your love life, which to date consisted of dry-humping Karen Brigsby on the grassy summit of Eagle Cliff. But that didn't seem very romantic. You shrugged and said:

No one special.

What about Vivian? Have you been seeing much of her?

Not much, you answered. In fact you hadn't seen Vivian at all. When not working with your father in the Building you'd spent most of the summer with George and your mutual friends, riding your bicycles, hiking, and swimming at Huntington's. When not doing those things, you spent most of your time alone in your basement room, drawing in a sketchbook, or in the backyard, doing curls, bench presses, and Navy lifts with a rusty set of barbells that a friend (who never used them) gave you. Whenever you used them (in a determined effort to expunge the scrawniness from muscles that hadn't yet gotten the news that you were a man), the barbells sounded like an antique printing press.

At fifteen your arms were more muscular. Your neck was thicker, your shoulders were broader. You'd grown an inch. You dressed differently, too. You'd traded your pointy cowboy boots for square-toed Frye boots. You wore turtlenecks or cable-knit sweaters over crisp bell-bottoms, the front pockets of which you'd hook your thumbs into when you walked as the teacher had walked, with long determined strides and a pigeon-like forward thrust of your head. It never occurred to you that your imitation of the teacher was obvious. Or maybe it did, but you didn't care.

THE TEACHER PARKED the Karmann Ghia by the service road. From there you walked into the park. It was a gypsy moth plague year. Through the spring their ghostly tents had sprung up all over the woods. When summer arrived, swarms of black inchworms burst out of them to munch their way through the forests, turning verdant hills smoke gray as the worms stripped them bare. On perfectly cloudless days the worms' droppings made a sound exactly like falling rain.

You hiked off the main trail to the swimming rock, a large rock brooding over the water, where, without hesitation or shame, you took off your clothes and skinny-dipped out to a small island with a stone decorative lighthouse on it, your feet kicking up white plumes of water. You took turns climbing and jumping off the light-house. Afterward you lay stretched out on a smooth stone at its base, catching your breaths, drying under the sun's warm rays.

The sun sure feels good, you said as you lay there.

As thermonuclear devices go it has its charms, said the teacher.

You lay that way for some time, your eyes closed, listening to each other's breaths and to bird songs and the wind sighing through tree branches, the sun painting brilliant masterpieces on your eyelids. In the silence you heard another sound: the gentle rain of caterpillar droppings.

So how come you didn't write to me? you asked.

I wanted to, Peter. Believe me, I did. There were times when I had to fight back the urge to pick up a pen or the telephone.

What stopped you?

Time, said the teacher. I wanted to give you time. I felt you needed it.

Time for what?

Time to grow, to become the person you are now.

You let this sink in, or tried to.

How would your writing to me have stopped that?

I'm not sure it would have. It might not have made any dif-ference. But I didn't want to take any chances.

You nodded though you still didn't understand.

Maybe I should have written, said the teacher. Maybe it was presumptuous of me to assume that I was that important to you. What's important for you to know is that I was thinking less of myself than of you, Peter, wanting what was best for you. One thing I did know for sure, and that's that I didn't want to risk interfering in any way with your process of growing up. I'd done that already and regretted it.

What did you do?

I pushed you all too hard and fast. All of you, but especially you.

So? What harm did it do?

Perhaps a metaphor will help, the teacher said. And then he told you the story about the guru, his disciple, and the butterfly. Now do you understand? he asked.

I wasn't a caterpillar, and I'm not a butterfly.

No, but you were a boy and now you're a man. Anyway, whether or not I made the right decision in not writing you, I never for a moment doubted that we'd see each other again. I didn't mean for you to doubt it either, but I can understand why you did. And for that I'm sorry.

You went on talking then, both of you, the teacher's whispers joining the sounds of wind and birds and caterpillar droppings as he told you more about the work he'd been doing, and some projects he hoped to take up in the future, including his wish to create some sort of community where thoughtful, intelligent, caring, and talented people from all parts of the world and walks of life could come together to teach, learn, and live.

That's been my long-held dream, the teacher said.

You mean like a school?

More than school, a community. A place where people wouldn't just come to teach and learn, but to live and grow, to nurture and help each other in other ways. And just to be together and give each other support and strength.

So there'd be a campus and buildings and all that stuff?

Sure, there'd be a building or buildings. And stuff. Gardens, fields. Barns for animals. A research laboratory. A theater. A yoga center. Who knows?

Sounds pretty ambitious.

It is – but why think small?

Where would you build it?

I'm not sure. As far from all the bullshit as possible.

It's gonna cost a lot of money, it sounds like.

That it will.

Where will you get it – the money?

The teacher shrugged. I don't know. I haven't gotten to that yet. All I know is that there are a lot of people in the world who would be willing to help, who still know how to think and dream, who still have ideals. People like you and me. Some of these people have money or access to it – lots of it. And there's plenty of land available, unexploited land, some of it not terribly expensive. With perseverance and patience it can be done. Especially patience. Which is why I don't intend to rush things.

When do you plan to start?

When the time is right. The first step will be to find the right piece of land. I've already done a bit of research. I'm leaning toward the west coast, specifically the Pacific Northwest. The climate there's a lot gentler than it is here in the east. It rains a lot, but it's a gentle, relaxing rain. And there's plenty of undeveloped property. There's also a much more progressive culture out there. I hope to get out there soon to do some exploring. In the next year or two.

I'd like to be part of it, you said.

You will be. Don't worry.

YOU WERE HEADED back to the teacher's car when a mosquito landed on his arm.

Here, watch this, he said.

You watched as the teacher clenched the muscles of his forearm, trapping the mosquito as it sucked his blood. The mosquito's body filled with blood, growing bigger and bigger. At last it exploded, shooting a thin streak of blood across the teacher's forearm.

That's what happens, said the teacher as he wiped the blood away, when you hold on too long.

* * *

TWO MONTHS LATER, YOU RECEIVED THE FIRST OF MANY letters from the teacher. It arrived in a square envelope with a

Boston, Massachusetts, postmark, written in neat blue handwriting on a stationary card with a drawing of a boy gazing out at a sailboat sailing against a landscape of snow-peaked mountains.

Summer has come to an end and winter is just around the corner. Among a few select and dear human beings you lie heavily on my mind today. A mixture of frustration (the distance) and impatience (the time until) temper my thoughts....

Over the next few years many more letters followed, some on thin blue airmail stationary, some from as far away as India and Japan. They arrived at unpredictable intervals and never when you expected them. Months passed with no letters at all, then two would arrive in the same month.

... I'm finally back on my feet, recovered from travels and illness, moving slowly but with confidence toward the long cherished dream of starting a community, a place where people like us can live and work and teach together. The time is not yet ripe. Still, events seem to be heading toward the proper conditions.

Some of the letters were adorned with grace notes: a scrap of a dried chamomile flower pasted into a margin, a watercolor sketch of a backpacking hiker with walking stick, a sketch of a pine tree in green felt marker.

I'm amazed at the amount of pent-up emotion your letters project. I also get the feeling you're relentless with yourself. My first instinct is to wish you were here, to calm you down a bit and sooth away some of the loneliness by sharing. It's my further feeling that you've yet to experience an all-encompassing love, a relationship physical, emotional, and intellectual that empties you, letting some peace settle in.

You lived for those letters. Receiving one was like having your own life delivered to you in a stamped envelope.

The man writing this isn't the one you knew. He died a while ago, Peter, on a mountaintop in Nepal. It was a slow, agonizing death....

You'd wait for your papa to pedal his rusty Raleigh back from the post office, then check the mail in his handlebar basket for an envelope with your name and address in the teacher's handwriting.

Shit, Peter, I lie awake daydreaming of how wonderful this world could be for all of us, feeling like a man lying next to the most beautiful woman his heart or mind could ever conjure, but who's lost his balls to a society that doesn't know the difference between good and evil and doesn't give a fig. Blind people in a land of the blind – mute, begging for vision, using sign language I can't see or understand. At times I wish I were one of the multitude who won't ever know the difference as they fuck away in roles that other people cast them in. Maslow must have been out of his fucking mind! Does anyone ever really self-actualize? The great gardener in the sky had already weeded all the true selves out of the garden the moment the first tender shoot dared to whisper "I am!"...

Now and then the letters conveyed a note of dismay or disapproval with respect to something you'd said or done, or an unworthy thought, opinion, or belief.

Another part of me thinks, Bullshit! Trite bullshit! Why bother to write? Who is this Peter you haven't seen in years? What kind of silly fool am I to resurrect old memories that should have died long ago, waking memories of those dried out little turds – Bethel personified – who made my life a living hell in that tunnel-visioned environment in which I was once a prisoner. A powerful bomb dropped in its center wouldn't bring the semblance of a tear to my eyes. Damn it, Peter, I don't want to be relegated to a shit-pile of old memories!....

But mostly the letters were encouraging, offering words of praise, giving advice or reassurance, brimming with hope for the future, for the community the teacher hoped to build – for Castalia, or what you had come to think of as Castalia, picturing a castle-like fortress on a mountaintop, surrounded by lakes, fields and farms, at an elevation so high most of the time it was hidden by clouds, so the ordinary people living down in the valley couldn't see it.

Dear of the great inquiring probing eyes, sensitive Peter, spiteful Peter, loving Peter... Peter so easily hurt and so easily hurting others. Know I love you, this one statement having the intensity of the entire human race chanting in unison, that that love is deeper than your postures at different stages, that it's for you as you continue to grow, as you were stages ago and will be stages to come and lifetimes to be. ...

* * *

FOLLOWING THE TEACHER'S SURPRISE SUMMER VISIT, through what remained of high school, you felt like an imposter, a grown man impersonating a pimply teenager. And though you played the part fairly well, getting along with friends and class-mates and earning decent grades, still, you felt woefully miscast, impatient for the greater roles that you felt destined to perform.

Meanwhile you lifted your rusty barbells, wrote, and sketched in the den that had been your grandmother's room, its odors of naphthalene, lilac, and soy sauce replaced by that of fresh paint. Nonnie was dead. She died in the nursing home where she spent her last days. One day, your father stopped by for a visit to find her gray cadaver lying there with its eyes open. He'd left you waiting in the parked car. Afterward, as he put the car into gear, an odd sound escaped him – half sniffle, half gasp. It was as close as you had ever come to hearing him cry.

Your father owned a Pinto now. It was his first American car. He had traded in his Simca for it. During junior year, while parked in the rain in the muddy yard of a burned-down hat factory, you lost your virginity in its front seat, a milestone whose legacies included a sore back, a bent gearshift, and your first case of crab lice.

GIVEN THAT YOU were already an actor, when a local commu-nity theater put up a casting notice for *Camelot,* you auditioned for the part of Sir Lancelot, King Arthur's favorite knight, doomed by his love affair with Guinevere. No sooner did the notice appear in the *Bethel Home News* than you ran out and bought the original Broadway cast album.

To prepare for the audition you practiced your songs while mowing the grass, the cracks in your voice drowned out by a 5-horsepower lawnmower engine.

Your diligence was rewarded. You got the part.

Guess who was cast as Guinevere?

By then you had a crush on Vivian, who was, after, all, your closest remaining link to the teacher. Those feelings you held for him that couldn't be conveyed in his absence, and certain other feelings as well, you directed toward her.

You had three weeks to rehearse. In your determination to reach the high E-flat in "If Ever I Would Leave You" (a number the musical director offered to transpose to a more comfortable key for you, which generous offer you declined) you took voice lessons from a private music coach.

The coach, whose name was Madame Yoffa, once toured with the National Opera Company of Vilnus, Lithuania, or so she claimed. A heavyset middle-aged woman, she lived with her three aging dachshunds – all blind, deaf, and prone to diarrhea – in a Victorian on South Street, next door to the Bethel Volunteer Fire Department.

Madam Yoffa wore colorfully embroidered peasant outfits befitting her bohemian past if not her age. Her breath was rankly sour, its sourness only partly explained by the empty vodka fifths in her kitchen trash. Without fail your sessions would be interrupted by the wail of the siren going off next door. While waiting for it to stop, you'd stand and Madam Yoffa would sit at her spinet piano, grimacing, eyes squeezed shut, her fingers in her ears, saying, *Ach – ven vill dey vinish do burn down, zo many houzes?*

Later, as you ran up and down the scales, she'd crouch behind you, squeezing your ribcage as though it were a concertina, saying, *Pooj* oud, *pooj* oud *wid yur lungz!* With each lesson Madam Yoffa's hands sank a little lower, until one day, as politely as you could, you indicated this to her. She vaulted from her sofa, shouting, *I know vat I'm doink! You tink I don't know vat I am doink?*

Normally at the end of your lessons Madam Yoffa would offer you homemade *kiffles* with a glass of milk. But that afternoon no kiffles were forthcoming and the lesson turned out to be your last.

DURING THE FINAL week of rehearsals, Vivian phoned to ask if you cared to run lines with her. In your new used car, a rusty MG with four different-sized tires that you'd bought for $200, you drove to her boxy raised ranch house in a development called Chimney Heights. As you were pulling into her driveway, Vivian stepped out of her front door. Carrying a plaid blanket, she marched up to your MG, got in, and slammed the rusty door.

Let's go, she commanded.

Where to?

Anywhere. As long as there are no goddamn people around.

You drove to Huntington State Park, the same park you'd gone to with the teacher. As you entered the woods, a chorus of cicadas sang the song of a muggy day. Through the overarching branches sunlight flickered, painting pale flowers on Vivian's cheeks. You carried both scripts, yours and hers. Vivian carried the plaid blanket.

Every dozen yards or so you came to what seemed to you a perfectly good place to run lines, but Vivian kept shaking her head, saying, *No; deeper.* She walked on ahead of you, turning every ten or so steps to cast you her sly Mona Lisa smile. One time, as she turned back, she collided with a mass of cobwebs leftover from the gypsy moth plague. The web formed a gossamer veil over her face that, like a groom preparing to kiss his bride, you lifted gently off.

Ugh, Vivian said.

Following a series of "deepers," you settled on a patch of moss between two trees. You spread out the plaid blanket. As Vivian sat on it with her legs crossed, you thumbed through your copy of the script, wondering where you should begin. You were thumbing it that way when suddenly Vivian grabbed it from you.

How about right here? she said, tossing the script over her shoulder and jamming her tongue hard and deep into your mouth. Breathlessly between tongue-thrusts she uttered:

We can do whatever you want. Just please don't come inside me. I don't want anything to do with your children.

You wore a denim cowboy shirt, the kind with pearl and metal snaps instead of buttons. As Vivian thrust herself into you, one of the snaps dug painfully into your sternum.

Hold on, you said.

Vivian tapped her fingers on the blanket as you fumblingly removed your shirt.

Okay, you said when you'd finished. I'm ready now.

Do you have a condom? Vivian asked.

A what? you said.

A condom. A rubber. You know what a rubber is, don't you?

Huh? Sure – sure I know what a rubber is, you said.

Have you got one?

Huh? Oh, I'm not sure. Wait, let me see …

You pretended to check your pockets.

This is hopeless, said Vivian, standing.

What's the matter?

I feel like a child molester!

Go on, you said. Molest me!

Having yanked the blanket out from under you, Vivian huffed off. She huffed all the way back to where you'd parked the car, streaming obscenities and snapping tree branches in your face all the way as you followed.

It's all your fault, she said.

What's my fault? What the hell are you *talking* about?

She climbed into the passenger seat.

Take me home, she said.

Not until you tell me what this is about!

Take me home, goddammit. *Now!*

You got in the car and turned the key. The starter wound and wound, losing power. Just when you thought it wouldn't, the engine turned over. Vivian got a cigarette from her purse and tried to light it using the dashboard lighter, which like so many things in the car didn't work. She tossed her unlit cigarette and the lighter into the parking lot.

Homo, she muttered as you backed the car out.

You slammed the brakes.

What?

Shut up and drive!

What did you say?

Vivian sat there with her arms crossed.

I'm not a homo!

You couldn't prove it by me.

Let's go back in the woods. I'll prove it!

Either you put this piece of shit of a car in gear and drive me home or I swear I'll make you rue the day you were born.

You pulled out of the parking lot.

As you drove her home Vivian sat stiff in the passenger seat, her arms folded over her still unbuttoned blouse, the nipple of one of her breasts – the one closest to you, the left one – exposed. Over the MG's winding roar and the noise of wind rushing over the windshield you tried to defend yourself against Vivian's charge, but she wouldn't hear it, cutting you off, saying, *One more peep out of you and I swear to God I'll steer this hunk of shit into the next tree!* You downshifted and floored the gas and white-knuckled the steering wheel, praying for an oncoming vehicle to crash into, picturing Vivian, her arms still folded across her chest, soaring ass-over-teakettle over the cracked MG windshield. But it was Sunday and the roads were empty. You made it safely back to Chimney Heights. As Vivian got out of the car you said:

I still don't have any idea what the hell all this is about!

I'll give you a clue, Vivian said, and spoke the teacher's name while slamming the car door.

What's he got to do with anything?

If not for you he'd still be here, that's what. It was thanks to you that he got fired – you and your latent homosexual puppy love!

As you sat with your jaw hanging, dragging the blanket with her, Vivian marched to her front door. When she reached it she stopped, turned, and yelled:

He loved me. That's right, asshole. We were in love. And now he's gone and I'll probably never see him again. All thanks to you, you little queer!

She stormed on into her house.

* * *

THROUGHOUT *CAMELOT'S* TWO-WEEK-LONG RUN, WITH the exception of King Arthur (whose part was played by a happily married carpeting and floor tile salesman), Vivian made-out with every male cast and crew member, including the other knights of the Round Table and King Pellinore. You'd catch them necking in the folds of a curtain, behind canvas flats, in the parking lot after a performance.

If that wasn't dispiriting enough, while you made love to her on stage, swearing in song that you'd never leave her in any season – not in summer, winter, fall, or spring (*oh no not in spriingtiiimmmmmme!*), Guinevere poured a stream of expletives into your downstage ear.

You never did reach that E-flat.

MY FATHER WAS AN EXTREME EXAMPLE OF A NON-BELIEVER, *a man who refused to attach himself to anyone – or any place, institution, system, God, etc., who wished to be ruled exclusively by the powers of his own reasoning. Yet in choosing to be, as it were, "his own invention," he denied his origins – a denial that was, paradoxically, irrational. His gods were truth and logic; yet his desire to uproot himself overwhelmed logic and truth.*

Though he spoke four languages fluently, his favorite language was German. He enjoyed its portmanteau compound nouns (Windschutzscheibenwischer = windshield wiper) as well as the sometimes complex, precise, and often untranslatable meanings that such words compressed (der Vorwärtseinparker: one who drives forward into a parallel parking space) – i.e., the very qualities of the German language most people find abhorrent. In the same spirit in which he embraced the lowly mice, rats, snakes, and spiders that took up residence in his laboratory, my papa embraced the scorned qualities of this "ugly" tongue.

Among my father's many unpublished manuscripts is one titled The Missing Words of Four Languages, *in which he does a comparative analysis of English, French, German, and Italian, discovering which words have no equivalents in certain languages. "Shadenfreude" is one such word; "simpatico" another. In his study, my father makes the case that where specific words are lacking so are the qualities that they describe. While an English speaker may occasionally feel something like "shadenfreude," he doesn't feel precisely what that term* means; the word does not translate, therefore neither does the emotion, and vice versa.

I wonder if something of the sort is true with respect to heritage, if certain attributes and emotions are lost in translation – if, for instance, in translating himself from Italian to English, my father sacrificed certain of his qualities, and in forsaking his Jewish origins he sacrificed others. Of course, a new language presents new opportunities, and the loss didn't come without gains. But as Papa demonstrates in his book, what's lost in translation can at best be approximated.

By filling in some of the holes in the past – my father's, the teacher's, my own – I'm hoping to reclaim some of what's been lost in translation.

* * *

PAPA'S DOG FOOD EPISODE. MOTHER SUFFERING FROM migraine, having one of her attacks. Dr. Mandel came with his kit to give her a shot of morphine. A few hours later, my mother asked my father for ginger ale. He brought her a glass. Later, she became hungry and asked him to bring her a bowl of cereal and milk. A short while later, she heard a crash. Papa appeared at the threshold of Mom's bedroom holding a gallon jug of milk, a spoon, and an upside down box of what he'd thought was cereal, but was in fact the dog's food, which had fallen out of the inverted box as he climbed the stairs, the cereal pellets spilling down them like a waterfall. Sick though she was, my mother spent the next half hour picking up pellets of dry dog food while my father watched the evening news.

My mother told me that story as well as one about how Papa would help her rake the leaves. Seeing her hard at work, raking and carting off enormous bundles of leaves, Papa would volunteer to lend a hand. He'd fill one blanket half full of leaves, claim he had urgent business to attend to down in the Building, and that would be that.

We laugh at these stories now, my mother and I, though at the time for her they couldn't have been very funny. Strange, isn't it, how in retrospect when speaking of the dead bad behavior inspires affection.

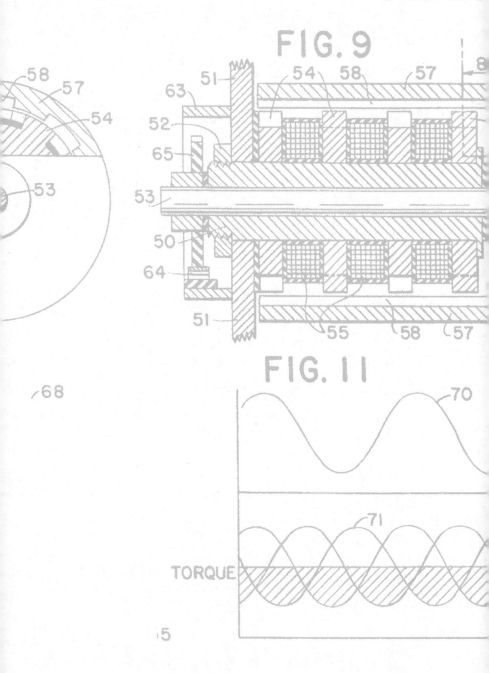

FIG. 9

FIG. 11

TORQUE

From Patent No. 3,387,151, "ELECTRIC MOTOR": An end view of the motor showing the three pairs of contacts and the cam wheel which operates them. This view also shows a schematic wiring diagram."

XIII.
The Touch
New York City, 1977

THE NEXT TIME YOU SAW THE TEACHER YOU WERE AN art student living in New York City, a city you loved ever since you were six years old, when your papa took you there with him for the first time on one of his so-called "business trips."

Remember those trips to New York City with your papa? Never mind: I'll do it for you.

YOU'D LEAVE ON Friday mornings. The trip took just a little over an hour, but you might as well have been taking off for Pluto or Neptune, it seemed so very far. As your father backed the Simca around the white birch in the turnaround you'd see your mother and your brother standing there, next to the garage, your mother waving, your twin brother crying, as you would cry next Friday when it would be George's turn.

You rode past the War Memorial, the Danbury fairgrounds, the Dinosaur Gift & Mineral Shoppe, with its pink stucco tyrannosaurus. The Interstate had yet to be built, so you took the Saw Mill River Parkway. Past reservoirs, orchards, and nurseries you rolled, through Katonah, Chappaqua, Pleasantville, tallying bridges and groundhogs.

Your father hummed the *Blue Danube* and sang Maurice Chevalier songs, his Kent cigarette dangling, his arm out the window, preferring it to the turning signal, his other hand steering, its knuckles stained with metal grime. The Simca's glove compartment burst with service station roadmaps, but he never consulted them.

The city's outskirts were a tangle of parkways, thruways, express-
ways, toll roads, and turnpikes; that your father could untangle
them amazed you. But then they seemed to belong to him, those
tangled highways, as did everything to do with New York City.

At the Henry Hudson Bridge he'd toss a nickel into the toll
basket. You rolled under the girders of the George Washington
Bridge. Here the city began in earnest. The Cloisters, Grant's Tomb.
Among drab shapes in the distance patches of color appeared, the
bright funnels of ocean liners in their berths. To your left, a skyscraper garden flourished, the Empire State Building a deco fountain rising from its center. Amid the architectural profusion a giant
fuel storage tank proclaimed GAS HEATS BEST.

Then the elevated ended; the Simca descended into a shady
jungle of bumpy cobblestones. Along Canal Street your father
parked. Gripping your hand he led you from one industrial sur-
plus shop to another, foraging parts for his inventions. The faces
that crowded the sidewalks were like the baubles on a Christmas
tree. There were few dogs and fewer children. The city was a place
for grown-ups.

From Canal Street you walked to Chinatown, where you
ducked into shops packed with lacquered trays and jade carvings.
There the streets smelled of fish. In one of those shops, your father
bought you a carved wooden box. (I still have it; it sits on a bookcase next to the desk where I write.) In Chinatown the plethora of
street signs held you spellbound, transformed into adornments
by virtue of being illegible. They clung there, butterflies caught in
a lightless tangle of fire escapes and utility lines.

In Greenwich Village the boutiques teemed with trinkets,
boxes, beads, and reeked of incense. The city was a colossal museum of objects divided into galleries according to periods and styles.
Its purpose: to amuse you.

You returned to the Simca and drove back uptown, stopping
for lunch at Schrafft's, then on to Manganaro's Italian Import Store
to buy your mother some parmesan cheese, the jagged hunk broken off a heavy golden wheel. Then up West End Avenue to Nine-

ty-sixth Street, where your father parked the Simca not far from your hotel. After checking in, you and your father rode the subway back downtown.

It was mid-September, but the subway platform still hoarded summer heat. The station's dim lighting gleamed off its innumerable tiles. A man in a dark gray suit leaned against a pillar. Others stooped over the tracks. None said a word. You obeyed the unwritten law by which New Yorkers pretend to ignore each other. A muffled roar heralded the subway train's arrival. The roar grew so deafening you plugged your ears. Then the train squealed to a stop and its doors slid open.

Clinging to straps, you and your papa careened underneath the city, the subterranean world a murky blur punctuated by lustrous stations whose waiting faces looked on in envy while you roared by on express tracks. You rode the subway to the Battery, where gulls wheeled over the ferry that you rode to the Statue of Liberty. Then back uptown to Union Square, where you jumped over the set of iron teeth that stretched to fill the platform gap. Then up a maze of latticed stairways into the dimming dusk.

From there you walked to the colossal pinball machine known as Times Square. In the settling darkness the lurid lights sold everything from Pepsi-Cola to convertible sofas. A giant Phil Silvers as Sergeant Bilko blew smoke rings into the electrified dusk. At an establishment called Nedick's you ordered two frankfurters with paper cups of papaya juice and watched traffic and pedestrians go by.

From Times Square you rode a taxi back to the hotel. Of all the city's features, the Hotel Paris was your favorite, a wedding-cake-shaped building of garnet colored brick topped by a crenelated turret, with a tall flagpole reaching farther up into the sky. The lobby was made of pink marble, with a mirrored dining room adjacent to it and an old-fashioned caged elevator whose diminutive black operator wore her flame-red hair in an immense beehive. She let you man the controls, a courtesy for which you would never forget her. It had to be done just right or the floors wouldn't align. She placed her brown hand over yours, its warm grip guiding. At every floor, the elevator's caged doors opened to different hallway carpeting, arabesques of brilliant color whose elaborate intricacies mirrored the teeming chaos outdoors.

Like all the Paris's rooms, yours was small and stuffy. It stank of the previous occupant's cigarettes, which was okay with you. You accepted the smell as part of the city – your father's city, so it seemed to you, as if he had laid every brick and cobblestone and built every skyscraper. As he unpacked his suitcase you watched, mesmerized. A suit, two pair each of socks and underwear, a can of foot powder, his battered shaving brush, his safety razor, a shoehorn, a necktie.

The necktie fascinated you most. You had seen it before, many times, hanging in your papa's closet back home. But in that hotel room it took on an entirely new aspect. With its paisley lemon drops against a maroon background it was no longer just your papa's tie. It was his New York City tie.

That tie became the city for you, as did the stale smell of that hotel room, and the gaudy hallway carpeting, and the black elevator operator, and the passenger ships snug in their berths, and the GAS HEATS BEST slogan on the side of a fuel storage tank that could have been the imperative of an almighty God. It was all part of the city that belonged to him, to your inventor papa, who'd invented it for you, his son.

* * *

AFTER HIGH SCHOOL YOU WEREN'T SURE WHAT YOU wanted to do. While George and your mutual friends went off to college, you took a job with a furniture company, delivering dry sinks, dining hutches, grandfather clocks, and sleeper sofas to homes in the tri-state area. As driver's helper you weren't supposed to drive, but Al, the official driver, let you. Sitting behind the wheel of a forty-five-foot truck in your green Ethan Allen uniform made you feel manly, a compensation of more value to you than your salary. You'd take your sketchpad to work and sketch Al and the rest of the warehouse crew to mixed responses.

You did that job for a year, after which you made up your mind to study art in the city that you loved. At the art school in Brooklyn, you took courses in drawing, painting, illustration, graphic design, theater, and film. And though your interest in each of these subjects was sincere, you still really had no idea what you wanted to do. All you knew was that you wanted to be an artist of some kind – a famous one, preferably, someone recognized and admired for his bold, unique style.

In a word, you wanted to be special. By then that need was so deeply ingrained in you it felt like an imperative, something you could no more escape than you could escape growing old and dying. It was your destiny.

The need to be special set you apart from others if not at odds with them. The alternative would have been fitting in, and fitting in meant, among other things, admitting to yourself that you were no better than the people around you, meaning they were no less special than you. In judging them, you would have to apply the same standards you applied to yourself. You would have to compete with them on the same grounds, to play by the same rules. You'd have to be treated equally, as you and your twin brother had once been treated as equals – a prospect that, consciously or otherwise, you found as inviting as that of sharing your mother's womb again.

THE FRIENDS YOU made while in art school tended to be other alienated souls unwilling or unable to run with the crowd. There was the handsome Puerto Rican painting and theater major. He did a three-dimensional painting once of a dead bird in a coffin. He used an actual dead bird that he'd found and sprayed with Krylon varnish, and that – in spite of this – gave off a faint nasty odor whenever you raised the coffin lid.

There was the Vietnam veteran turned assemblage artist and filmmaker. One of his collages featured a hundred Marlboro cigarette packs arranged in a grid and splattered, a lá Jackson Pollock, with blood-red enamel paint. With him you made short films about drug addicts, psychopaths, and lobotomy patients in which you would star, and went on to do storyboards, wrangle props, build and dress sets, and design posters for other people's movies (including people of low, if not criminal, repute).

Nor did you lack for relationships with the opposite sex, though these tended to be catch-as-catch-can. At a loft party – or was it a gallery opening? – in Soho – or was it Chinatown? – you met a woman named Gretta – or was it Gertrude? You hailed a taxi and rode it to her basement dwelling on the Lower East Side, or was it Alphabet City? The dwelling's windows were barred. It featured a caged sulfur-crested cockatoo that squawked, *"I'm so pretty! I'm so pretty!"* while its owner and you made love.

You drew, painted, wrote, auditioned for parts. One day you auditioned for a singing waiter job at a Third Avenue restaurant. The accompanist refused to transpose "On the Street Where You Live" to your key. They hired you to work in the kitchen instead, manning a huge stainless steel console with steaming tureens holding different-colored sauces. As singing waiters hurried in and out of the kitchen, you handed them the plates of fish, beef, or chicken over which you'd ladled the different sauces. Halfway through your first shift, in your exhaustion and confusion, you began putting the red sauce on the fish and the tan sauce on the beef and the brown sauce on the chicken. They fired you.

Some weeks later you were cast as an extra in a movie whose famous comic director wore plaid shirts and horn-rimmed glasses. Along with the others who had been selected from a three-city-block-long cattle call, you were ushered into a cavernous room and told to sit against one of two walls. It would take you many years, until you finally saw the movie, to grasp the purpose of this bifurcation. In a famous scene in the movie the main character (played by the comedian director) sits glumly in the car of a passenger train filled with grim, miserable-looking people. As he sits there another train pulls up alongside his, this one filled with happy, smiling, attractive people throwing a party. As he watches from his stalled sad train the happy train leaves the station.

And though apparently you had been cast in the "happy

train," you were never in the movie, having attended the costume fitting and two days of rehearsal only to miss the day of the actual shoot thanks to a faulty alarm clock. (The comic director is known, incidentally, for having said, "Half of success is showing up.")

Through these and other experiences you felt the hand of fate casting its shadow over you, waiting to pluck you from obscurity and deliver you to your true destiny, to either some form of artistic fame and fortune, or to Castalia, the community of intelligent, like-minded, idealistic souls that the teacher planned to create.

While waiting, you carried a sketchbook with you everywhere. At cafe tables, on street corners, at gatherings with friends, you'd fill its pages with sketches and writing. Over the next ten years you filled more than a dozen sketchbooks. You stored them on shelves in the different apartments where you lived. Pressed for space, you mailed them to your mother, who stored them for you in the basement of the house where you grew up.

THE INNOCENT CITY, the one you so loved when your father took you there with him as a child, the city of Christmas tree skyscrapers and bright-funneled ocean liners no longer existed. A darker city had taken its place: a greedy, lusty, brutish, grueling city. A fire-breathing dragon that consumed innocence and exhaled ambition and alienation.

Unlike the New York City of your childhood and adolescence, this New York confused you. Confronted by its maze of doors and passageways, any one of which might lead you to your destiny, you were paralyzed with indecision, knowing that in choosing one path you'd cut off all the others. So you didn't – couldn't – choose.

Now and then on a busy street corner you would be so gripped by paralysis you'd be unable to decide which way to cross. You'd stand there, frozen as the other pedestrians jostled you, cursing under their breaths but loudly enough for you to hear. You had learned your way around the city only to find yourself directionless there.

This lack of impetus begot awkward situations, like the time you ran into that English fellow on the corner of Eighth Street and Astor Place. He said he was an actor with the Old Vic, in town to do a production *Macbeth*. Since he looked like Richard Basehart you believed him. You had no hair. You'd shaved it down to peach fuzz. For some reason, this provoked and inspired gay men. Macbeth wondered where "a bloke from out of town" could get "a bloody drink." It was the winter of your second year of art school. You were still living in Brooklyn, renting a room in the brownstone of a retired church choir conductor. You weren't knowledgeable with respect to Manhattan bars and said so. This didn't dissuade Macbeth. You ended up having bloody marys at Chumley's, and from there went to Macbeth's place, the borrowed "flat" of some other actor. Having mixed each of you a screwdriver, Richard Basehart lay on his back on the parquet floor and fondled himself while reciting explicit passages from Henry Miller. He didn't notice or seem to care when you stepped over him and out the door.

Another time, during a snowstorm that blew on your twenty-first birthday, a former Presbyterian minister who had taken you out to dinner invited you to spend the night at his loft, which you did, gladly, having come to detest those two a.m. subway trips back to Brooklyn. As the former clergyman fellated you, you pretended to be somewhere else enjoying the ministrations of a different set of tongue and lips. The next morning, your host was beside himself. You told him to forget about it. Honestly, you said, I couldn't care less. You meant it, too. What did you care if some former clergyman sucked you off? It's not like it hurt or anything. (Implicit in this denial was the distinction between sex and emotions, a dichotomy of which you would be largely oblivious but that would inform your romantic relationships for years to come, for much of your adult life.)

During those first years in the city you kept having a recurrent dream, a nightmare, one that parachuted you down into the city's combat zone, amid its vaporous lights and alleyways. In the dream you'd always end up at a movie theater, one of those sordid theaters near Times Square, attached to an un-deployed army of men wearing London Fog coats and hunched in their seats. You faced a screen on which the images were tantalizingly out of focus, looking more like Cézanne's peaches than human bodies engaged in carnal acts. But the soundtrack was clear: a moan is a moan is a moan. In the dream, as if by your own tumescence, you would levitate out of your folding seat toward a neon sign pulsing over the door to a lavatory behind which ultimate depravities lay in wait for you, tinged with ultraviolet light, perfumed by stale urine.

Debased by your own dreams.

This was the New York City to which you had returned.

* * *

ONE WINTRY AFTERNOON IN LATE DECEMBER 1976, IN the same rusty Karmann Ghia (incongruous in the snowy streets of Brooklyn) that you'd gone to Huntington Park together in, the teacher arrived. You helped him find a parking space, then rode the subway into Manhattan, where you toured the museums: the Metropolitan, the Cooper-Hewitt, the Frick. At the Guggenheim, you balked at the price of admission: three bucks to penetrate a colossal Carvel ice-cream cone! Screw it!

You walked farther uptown. In Harlem the streets were in every sense browner, its buildings slung low to accommodate a sky brought to its knees by brawny gray clouds. A sudden whirlwind whipped grit into your eyes. It started to rain. Hunkered into it, you walked faster, the gusts flapping the lapels of your winter coats, past a building shaped like the parabolas you learned about in Mr. Proli's algebra class.

From Harlem you doubled back through Central Park, past Rockefeller Center and Radio City to Times Square, where, as a light snow fell, you passed under a succession of marquees featuring porno movies and 25¢ peep shows, a Coney Island of sex. From a shadowy threshold two heavily made-up women emerged to offer you a good time.

Thanks but no thanks, said the teacher.

We're having a good time already, you informed them.

From there you went to the Village, where you toured the same boutiques that you and your papa had toured fourteen years previously. At the corner of Thompson and West Third Street you stopped to admire the window display of a chess store, with its armies of chess pieces in rosewood, jade, ebony, alabaster, and malachite. While looking at them the teacher told you about the Café de la Régence in Paris.

Diderot set *Rameau's Nephew,* his masterpiece, there, he said.

Huh.

From Greenwich Village you crossed through ice and slush to the East Side, where you dined at a Ukrainian restaurant. The waiters were old men in ochre waist-cut jackets who scowled while taking your orders for *varenyky* and stuffed cabbage.

By the time you stepped back out of the subway station in Brooklyn it was dark and snowing heavily. Two black children, one wielding a bicycle pump, chased each other through the snow down a dark side street. On another street a woman chipped away at the ice on her stoop with the bent lip of a snow shovel, which caught the glimmer of a streetlamp. You had started toward the teacher's Karmann Ghia when he asked you if he might spend the night at your place.

If it's all the same with you, he said, I'd rather not have to drive in this weather.

You're welcome to stay, you told him.

Are you sure?

Absolutely. No problem.

Only as you approached the apartment building where you rented a room from a retired church choir conductor did it dawn on you that you had only one bed and no sofa, and that bed a mattress you'd dragged in off the street and shoved into a corner on the floor, near a bookshelf packed with paint in jars and tubes and coffee cans bristling with brushes. Nearby were more cans of inexpensive house paint that you used when you couldn't afford oils or acrylics. Leaning against the room's walls were rolls of canvas and wooden stretcher bars tied into bundles with twine. In a corner stood a flimsy easel holding a large, half-finished canvas. Subject: a fishmonger slicing the head off a fish. Next to the fishmonger, sharing the same plane with it, an oil-drum fire blazed. In the background more fishmongers stood silhouetted by the flames of other, smaller oil-drum fires.

That painting was the first thing the teacher saw when he entered your room.

Your latest? he asked.

Yeah. But I'm gonna paint it over.

Why?

I'm not happy with it.

Why not?

You shook your head. The drawing's off, for one thing.

The teacher stepped closer and studied the painting, his head cocked slightly to one side, his fingers playing over its surface. He said:

Don't – don't paint over it. Leave it. Just as it is.

But it's a mess.

Says who?

I do.

And I say it's perfect just as it is.

Come off it!

Rather than paint it over, why don't you sell it to me? I'd like to have it.

You're pulling my leg.

Name your price.

That piece of crap? You must be joking! At least let me paint you something good.

I want this one. I won't accept substitutes.

Fine, then take it. It's yours.

I insist on paying you for it.

And I insist on giving the damn thing to you. Do you want it or not?

In that case I accept.

WHILE THE TEACHER brushed his teeth you lay under the covers with the lamp on, staring up at the ceiling, feeling nervous. You understood that a decision was to be made, and that you'd be making it very soon. As you lay staring at shadows being chased across the ceiling by the headlights of passing cars you anticipated that moment when, in his underwear, the teacher would slide under the covers next to you. What happened next would be largely – if not entirely – up to you and would determine the shape and direction not only of your relationship with the teacher but of your future in many other respects.

And though you dreaded what you saw as, if not inevitable, a distinct possibility, you also knew that you would not resist, that your love for the teacher was such that it would overwhelm any form of resistance, that it would not be up to you, really, or anyway that you would not let it be up to you: you would not determine things one way or the other. You'd let him decide. That was your decision.

Having decided, you lay there, waiting. After what seemed like an extremely long time, the teacher came out of the bathroom and got into the bed next to you.

For a long time you lay there next to each other, with the table lamp switched off and the light of a streetlight spilling in through the blindless, curtainless window, both of you staring at the ceiling. Every few minutes a car or truck went by, its snow chains rattling, and together you watched the headlight beam chase another shadow across the walls. Neither of you moved. You heard the teacher's ragged breathing – or were they your own ragged breaths? You lay perfectly still, both of you, not touching each other, afraid to move, trying not to swallow or even to breathe. Scared to death.

The teacher's voice broke the silence.

May I – touch you? he said.

Sure. Go ahead.

Carefully, as if applying a poultice to a wound, the teacher placed his hand on your thigh. It felt cold and warm. Neither of you moved.

You lay there like that for at least an hour, listening to the sounds of traffic moving through the snow, watching the play of shadows and lights, scarcely breathing. You lay there that way until you fell asleep.

* * *

DISCUSSING THAT NIGHT WITH ONE OF MANY THERAPISTS whose services you would engage in the coming years, she'd say:

> *You have to forgive yourself.*
>
> *For what?*
>
> *For making your teacher reject you.*
>
> *How did I do that?*
>
> *By rejecting him first.*
>
> *When did I reject him?*
>
> *That night in your room.*
>
> *I didn't reject him. He asked if he could touch me and I said sure.*
>
> *And you lay there with his hand on you and did nothing. That hand was an invitation. You refused it. A passive refusal is still a refusal. You might as well have slapped him in the face. It's a wonder he ever spoke to you again.*
>
> *I left it up to him.*
>
> *Right, your therapist would say. And it was up to you. Whether or not you rejected your teacher is beside the point. In fact – if I may be frank – it seems to me quite clear that from the start your teacher's actions were inappropriate. He should never have let you get that close to him. He was grossly derelict of duty, and if he wasn't fired then he should have been. At best his behavior was ill-considered, at worst it was predatory.*
>
> *But it wasn't like that! He wasn't a bad man! He was a good man!*
>
> *Even good people sometimes do bad things. Whatever your teacher's intentions may have been, the fact is he didn't do right by you. He wanted something from you that you weren't prepared to give to him, and that he was either too timid or decent to take. He took advantage of your need to feel special, and seduced you into idealistic dreams that gave you hope – but it was a false hope. He gave you something*

to believe in, an ecstatic, quasi-religious belief, when you believed in nothing, when your hyper-rational father's atheism left you bereft of any faith. He filled that void in you. He played Christ to your Apostle, the Devil to your Faust. That was his crime, not his physical or sexual attraction to you. He interrupted your process of maturation and left you longing for an ideal that you and the world could never live up to. You have every right to be angry.

But I'm not angry – I'm not!

You should be.

I don't want to be!

No one wants to be angry. Being angry isn't any fun.

I'd much rather remember the good things.

And well you should. But those good parts cost you, Peter. They cost you dearly. They cost you your youth. You're still paying for them. You bought them on the installment plan. Let's hope you don't end up paying for the rest of your life.

IN A DRAWER OF MY FILE CABINET, AMONG BANK AND *credit card statements, tax returns and receipts, in a thick folder I keep the letters the teacher wrote me. I've kept them for decades. There are over fifty of them, all of them handwritten, many on thin blue airmail stationary, the handwriting style neither print nor cursive but a blend of both, with long descenders and gracefully looped f's and g's, neat and graceful on the unlined paper. I take them out, put on a pair of drugstore reading glasses, and re-read them all. After reading them I spread them across the floor of my loft.*

A second portfolio holds the letters my father wrote me. There are just as many, though they aren't handwritten but typed with two fingers on my father's portable black Royal typewriter. I read them as well.

Reading all those letters – my father's and the teacher's – takes me all morning. Apart from their contents, the letters amaze and shame by how much kindness and sympathy they express. Whatever their virtues and flaws, whatever else was true or not true about them, the men who wrote those letters cared for me very much. I didn't appreciate just how much they really cared; like many young people, I was too caught up in myself. Now I realize it and feel ashamed and full of regret.

Audrey's connection with my father, who she never met: how she speaks of him all the time as if they had been buddies. She told her mother a story that went something like this: "When you and Daddy and Nonnie weren't looking, I went up to heaven to play a ship game [?] with Daddy's daddy. While I was up there I met a little girl named

Pickle who was there looking for her mommy, whose name was Cabbage. Then I drove the car back down to Mommy. I drove very carefully."

It's funny how Audrey thinks of her grandfather, since whenever I'm with her I imagine myself at her age and how I felt about him then, how I loved being with him. I remember especially those trips he took me on to New York City, how I came to equate that city with him and, for that reason among others, fell in love with it.

I don't miss New York City, but I do think of it often. We're invented not only by the people we know and love but also by the places we visit and call home. As much as anyone or anything, New York is responsible for inventing me, for my having become – for better and worse – who I am.

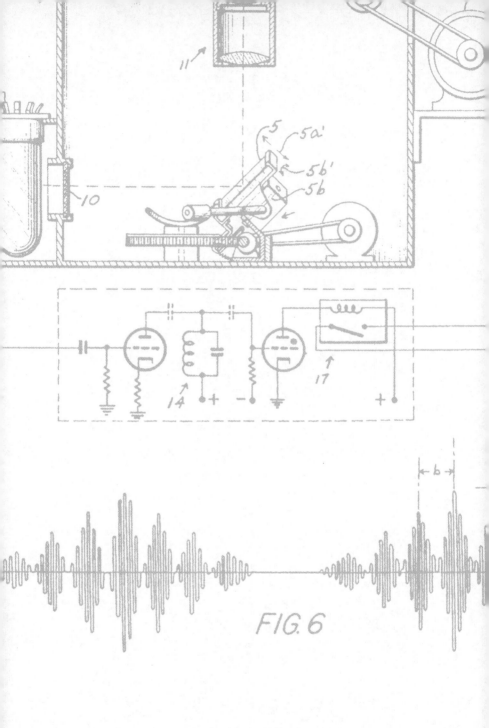

FIG. 6

From Patent Number 2,964,641: "A graph showing a typical group of recognition signals produced when an engraving is identified."

XIV.
The Boy on the Mountaintop
New Orleans, Annandale, New York City,
1977–1979

YOU WERE TWENTY-TWO YEARS OLD.

Now and then a letter arrived from the teacher. You would take it and your notebook to a park or a café, someplace where you could gather your thoughts and reflect and write him back – long letters, usually, some written under the influence of alcohol or marijuana. You'd go to Washington Square or Tompkins Square Park, buy a spliff, find a quiet bench, and write between tokes while keeping an eye peeled for cops.

Your father wrote you as well.

> *Dear Peter,*
> *I'm glad to have your letter to answer. I often feel the need to com-*
> *municate, to express my thoughts. I suppose it's what people mean*
> *about companionship. I don't have to tell you I'm very much alone. At*
> *times I feel it more than others...*

This and other letters from your father would eventually find their way into a folder in a drawer of your file cabinet, next to one holding the teacher's letters. But unlike the teacher's letters, despite their warm, self-deprecating humor, your father's letters vexed you. They filled you with the same anxiety you'd felt as a boy watching him enter various bodies of water – inch by painful inch, wincing and shuddering as though he were stepping into a vat of boiling oil.

> *This morning I had a frustrating experience. I had to prepare three*
> *Color Coders to be shipped by Monday at the very latest. Two were O.K.,*
> *but the third wouldn't work right. I replaced everything that could con-*

ceivably go wrong. I didn't know what to do. Finally I decided to build a circuit board from scratch with all new parts. It worked. To celebrate I bought a frame for one of my latest paintings. The sales girl there knows and asked about you, the one with red hair. I flirted with her, a 66 year-old man flirting with a girl of no more than 25. To be an old man is positively degrading.

Vulnerability and self-deprecation weren't what you wanted in a father, however sweetly expressed. What you wanted was someone to guide you with his firm grip and show you how to be a man in the world, someone to – speaking metaphorically – sling his arm around and take you fishing with him down at the ol' creek, like Sheriff Taylor in *The Andy Griffith Show*. Strength, resolve, determination, direction: all the qualities that you yourself lacked – they're what you wanted in a father. What you got were the saturnine sighs of a depressive old man:

I'm thinking of scrapping the paint box I made and buying a new one, lighter and better and not too expensive. Which reminds me: I have a new painting technique: squeeze colors onto a palette, then transfer bits of paint, still pure, to a second surface, mix as needed with a brush, then transfer to an even smaller palette or to paper to get the right consistency. Sounds complicated, but I think it will work better, less muddy.

Some day when, through a series of vicissitudes, you will have become the middle-aged man who writes these words, you will take all of your father's letters out of their folder and spread them out on the floor of the loft of the A-frame where you live – just as you'll do with the teacher's letters. You'll be shocked by how many letters there are, and by the vulnerability, sweetness, and warmth they express. By then your father will already have been dead for a decade. You'll miss him terribly, and you'll weep.

… The other day I went to the little park near the library to try out my new painting system. I brought a folding chair with me. I'd been sitting there for no more than five minutes when this silly old woman camped herself there in front of me and asked me about 46 questions. She wouldn't stop, nor would I answer.

"Why don't you answer me?" she said.

"Because I don't care to talk to you."

It worked: she left, and I convinced myself that it was the only way.

Then I started to wonder if maybe the reason I dislike pushy people is because I can't imitate them. It was because of things like this that my first wife Betty used to say I was a bad influence on our daughters. ...

But back when you first got them your father's letters vexed you, and your vexation turned to guilt for being so unappreciative of this man who, after all, was doing his best to love you. Was it his fault that he was depressed? Could he help it if he was born the same year the *Titanic* sank?

... I'm rambling, writing for myself more than for you. You do the same: it's good for us both.
    Love,
    Papa der Eber*

*German for boar, or wild pig. I love these German words that sound so totally unlike the things they mean. I also know I'm a very tame sort of pig, but I would love to be wild, with great crooked teeth.

* * *

THOUGH YOU ENJOYED PAINTING AND DRAWING, AND though a picture is said to be worth a thousand words, there were things you wanted to say that you couldn't say with pictures. So you decided to become a writer.

On the assumption that all writers did such things, you quit art school to hitchhike across the country. Your first ride took you all the way to Alabama, where your brother was an undergraduate at Auburn University, and where he offered to let you spend the night on the floor of his dorm room. While he went to class that afternoon you went to the library to write in your notebook.

George had a collection of antique fountain pens with solid gold nibs and handles of malachite, Bakelite, coral, jade, and amber. He'd been collecting them for years. Your nineteen-cent Bic pen had run out of ink. Without asking, you "borrowed" one of George's pens. You meant to return it, so you told yourself.

The next morning, seeing his fountain pen jutting out of a pocket in your backpack, your brother accused you of theft. He called you a "moocher" and a "libertine" – a word you had to look up later. You called him a greedy capitalist pig.

Hit the fucking road, your twin told you.

With tears in your eyes you crossed the foggy morning campus.

IN THE FRENCH Quarter of New Orleans a driver who'd gotten you stoned drove off with your backpack and all your traveler's checks. You paid $2.50 for a bunk in a flophouse, then joined the teenagers and tourists walking up and down Bourbon Street. At sunset, while eating an ice cream cone, you watched a barge lumber down the Mississippi.

You spent the rest of that summer in New Orleans, working at a cafe on the riverfront that served chicory laced *café au lait* and *beignets*.

You'd been working there for three days when you met a fellow waiter named Don, a small older man with a droopy handlebar mustache, thin black hair pulled into a ponytail and a space between his front teeth that gave him a lisp and made him sound drunk (as he probably was). Don offered to share his apartment with you, a small kitchen and equally small bedroom divided by a curtain of colorful Mardi Gras beads.

Shtep through my rainbow! said Don, parting them.

The place had only one bed.

True, said Don. But it's big and I'm small. I'm sure we'll both fit.

Your first night there, you awoke to Don's shiny forehead bobbing in the darkness over your groin. You pushed him off the bed. He apologized. After that, things were fine and you and Don became friends.

EVERY SO OFTEN Don's previous roommate, a junkie and hustler, would come looking for Don, hoping to trade sex for money. When Don refused him, his ex-roommate would beat and steal things from him. A few times you came home from your shift at the cafe to find him bleeding and bruised.

One night you awoke to what sounded like artillery fire. You got up and stood on the balcony, watching the Fourth of July fireworks paint huge chrysanthemums across the river. As you stood there you reflected on how much you'd changed. You were no longer the naïve, innocent kid from Connecticut, the oversensitive, needy boy with his umbilical cord still attached to his eighth-grade English teacher. At last, you said to yourself as Don lay snoring in the darkness behind you, I've become a man.

Just as you were thinking this you heard a rapping sound rising up the apartment's rickety stairs. Moments later, Don's ex-roommate stood before you. He wore the blouse of a Confederate uniform, its sleeves shorn, its bronze buttons dripping rainwater. His bare feet were filthy. He leaned on a cane.

Happy Fourth of Joolie!

By then Don was already in the bathroom, hiding. You sized up your opponent. He was exactly your height, with a thicker neck and broader sloped shoulders, his muscular arms filigreed with tattoos. He smelled of hot buttered popcorn. His face was sunburned the brown of glazed pottery. A wormy scar wriggled from his mouth to his ear. With his mop of curly hair he could have been your other twin, a cartoon version of you as dissolute drifter. He hummed a radio frequency from Mars.

Who the fuck are you?

I'm Don's roommate, you said. Don's not here.

He passed through the beaded curtain into the kitchen.

Believe this shit? Fourth of Joolie and the motherfucker's got no fuckin' beer.

You grabbed a paring knife from the drawer and gripped it. Like a child scrutinizing a worm in a terrarium, Don's ex-roommate eyed it. He hiked up his uniform blouse and touched his washboard belly to the knife's tip.

Go on: stick me! No? That case, put it away or someone's likely to get hurt.

With a Coke from the fridge he sat at the kitchen table, his cane propped against a chair. He lit one of Don's cigarettes. You still held the paring knife. You didn't know what to do with it. You had never stabbed anyone or come close to trying. You were still the naïve, sensitive kid from Connecticut. The paring knife trembled in your fist.

Someday, in a fictionalized rendering of this encounter, you'd lunge at your antagonist, wrestle him to the floor, and pound his scarred filthy face. In that version of this story, hearing the cries of his ex-roommate, Don would burst out of the bathroom and, grabbing the cane, send you – the nice kid from Connecticut – running "blind with terror" out into the unanimous wet night.

What actually happened:

Shouting, *What's matter? Forget what your face looks like?* Don's ex-roommate banged on the bathroom door with his cane. Don came out. They argued. When you tried to intervene, Don gave you some change from his tip apron and sent you out to the corner deli for a bottle of cheap red wine and a jar of pickled pig's feet. *Do me that favor, Peter, would you, please?*

When you returned, the beaded curtain was in tatters, its bright beads scattered everywhere. Don lay sprawled across his bed, bleeding and weeping.

My rainbow! He tore down my rainbow! That bastard! That son of a bitch!

A few days later, on a blend of tip money and donations from fellow waiters, you flew home, the French Quarter a postage stamp in the DC-9's window.

* * *

BACK IN THE NORTHEAST, YOU TRANSFERRED TO A SMALL private liberal arts college on the bank of the Hudson River an hour's drive north of New York City. You studied writing and literature. Having confronted bums, heroin addicts, and drunken homosexuals, you felt qualified to render human experience through words.

You had paid your dues; you had struggled. That most of your struggles were self-generated and therefore didn't count, or counted only so much, you failed to recognize or appreciate.

Thus you applied yourself to the writer's vocation, the latest in a long line of artistic flirtations. This time, however, you felt that your resolve would hold.

You weren't much of a student. When it came to your own initiatives, you applied yourself with ardor, working deep into the night. But for assigned labors you showed little initiative, preferring to do push-ups and sit-ups on the campus quad.

You were prone to distractions, chief among these being a coed with a French first name. She wore flowing white dresses and spoke in a permanent whisper – owing, perhaps, to the amount of time she spent in the library, bent over in her carrel in ardent pursuit of *Paradise Lost.*

How you loved Marie-Claude, and how she loved Albert, the Polish poet, who was fucking Cecilia, who had a crush on you. You knew that Cecilia was fucking Albert because he lived in the dorm room above yours, where you heard them fucking. That Marie-Claude's affection for Albert wasn't returned in kind didn't by the slightest degree extinguish her flame for him. Nor did it boost your prospects any.

In your bitter frustration you played Debussy (very loud) and shaved your hair off. You stopped eating and ran barefoot through snow and ice. You quit doing your school assignments and abandoned your latest novel-in-progress. On sunny days you sunned yourself in the same quad where you'd done push-ups and sit-ups, eyes closed, watching the patterns that the sun made under your eyelids as you once did with the teacher on the island with the decorative stone lighthouse. Ages ago, so it seemed.

One miserably cold winter afternoon as you were hitchhiking back to campus from the nearest town, you saw a car approaching, a car of Japanese make with rusted fender wells that you recognized as Marie-Claude's. You stood there smiling with your thumb out, waiting for her to see you and stop. Instead Marie-Claude drove right past you, her eyes fixed dead ahead – glued, no doubt, to the specter of the Polish poet.

A WEEK LATER you quit college and returned to New York City. You'd decided to be an actor again. You got the tip about the casting director from your personal manager, who warned you that he was a "slimebucket," but also said he was one of the biggest in town. If he liked you it would be a boon to your career.

Punctually at four p.m. you arrived at the casting agent's Hell's Kitchen apartment. The casting agent's assistant – a skinny boy probably not younger than you, but whose effeteness made him look younger – took your headshot and resumé and had you sit in the foyer. Minutes later the casting agent appeared – a plump, round-shouldered man in his seventies, wearing a gold satin bathrobe. You stood and introduced yourself.

The casting agent had a thick eastern European accent. *Sze James Dean dipe,* he remarked having looked you over, *but viz un Idalien tvist. Randy, holt my galls vuh ze nexd hefowr.*

The casting agent escorted you to his living room, the walls of which were papered with flocked red velveteen *fleurs-de-lis.* The heavy curtains were drawn, the lights were dimmed. Mahler's *Kindertotenlieder* played on the stereo. In the center of the room was an overstuffed white sofa on which the casting agent sat. From there in his thick accent he guided you through an exercise known as The Boy on the Mountaintop.

Ze berbus uf ze eggserzise, the casting agent explained, *iss do bring oud ze innozent liddle boy in yooh, ze vulnrable, innozent, helblezz liddle boy.*

The casting agent told you to picture yourself on a mountaintop. It is nighttime, he explained in his thick accent. You are all alone on the mountain under a blazing canopy of stars. Among all the stars is one star brighter than all the others.

I vunt yooh do reej voh zat briedest uv ztahs, the casting agent instructed.

You closed your eyes and reached. *Zat's ryed,* you heard the casting agent say, *reej voh it, reej voh zhe bruydest ztah! Yooh ken do id! Yooh ken! Yooh ken!* With your eyes still closed you reached as far as you could, so far you thought you would dislocate your arm.

Meanwhile the casting agent sat there on his white sofa, a fat-kneed god on an upholstered cloud, saying, *Yooh ken do it, yooh ken do it, yooh ken, yooh ken …*

While reaching for the star you heard a shuffling sound followed by the scratch of a needle being torn cruelly from a record.

Yooh kent, the casting agent's voice intruded. *Yooh kent duch ze stah. Yoohr ahms ah doo shzought. Yooh ah doo veek, doo szmall. Hits hobelezz. Yooh heffailed. Yooh ah a bed boy, a vey bed boy. Yooh neet do be bunished. Yooh neet do be shbanged …*

Dear Past Self, how I wish that I did not have to report what occurred next. How I wish I could say either that you were wise to the casting agent's subterfuge, but decided to go along with it for the hell of it, or that you didn't give a damn, or that, being such a fine actor, you were carried away by the exercise. The truth is less flattering. The truth is that you were too naïve, too cowed, too desperate for any form of success to do anything but obey.

So – with the needle replaced on the record, to the haunting strains of *der Kindertotenlieder,* beneath a dome of imaginary stars, you made your way to the casting agent, whose frowning knees poked out from under his gold satin robe, and draped yourself over his thighs. As his palm found you, you looked at the wallpaper, reading into its intricate forms the source of the pain that shot up to the level of your eyes before shivering down to the tips of your toes, imagining that it lay in the flocked red fleurs-de-lis and not in the casting agent's blows.

When you exited the casting agent's apartment building the sun was setting in lurid colors on the far side of the Hudson River. A harsh midwinter gust blew east across Fifty-fourth Street. Your cheeks burned from more than the cold. As you walked toward the subway you wondered if other actors had gotten their start this way, Brando, Dean, Cagney – if they too had endured The Boy on the Mountaintop or something like it. The thought made your cheeks burn hotter. You considered going back to the casting agent's apartment, punching his femmy assistant in the face, and choking the casting agent to death.

Instead you walked on to the subway station, slid a quarter under the token booth's Plexiglas partition, and sat with your head in your hands at the dark end of the platform, waiting for the downtown local.

The next morning you phoned your parents to say you were coming home.

BEFORE MEETING THE MOTHER OF MY CHILD I'D BEEN *married to another woman for seventeen years.*

Paulette lives in Nashville now. We're still friends; in fact, not long ago I stayed in her new home. I was passing through Tennessee on my way to Carbondale, Illinois, (Audrey's mother was attending graduate school there) to see my newborn, a journey of nine hours, and thought: why not? Her new beau, a guy named Duane she went to high school with, greeted me with her at the door. Nice guy. I liked him immediately. We ate dinner at a Greek restaurant, then I spent the night on the sofa in the living room of their condo that had so many of the trappings of our past marriage, from furniture to color schemes, I felt like an amnesiac who, after a protracted interval of lost wandering, had stumbled fortuitously back into his own forgotten life. Yes, it felt a bit weird. But like my father before me, I subjugated my raw emotions to reason. Why not feel just as (if not more) perfectly at home in the dwelling of my ex-wife and the man she loves as in a Motel 6?

In civilizing our feelings we sometimes do them and ourselves an injustice. It's better sometimes to not *be rational, to put our trust in more primitive feelings. This is something my father generally could not do and that I myself have a hard time doing. Among other things it makes falling in love hard.*

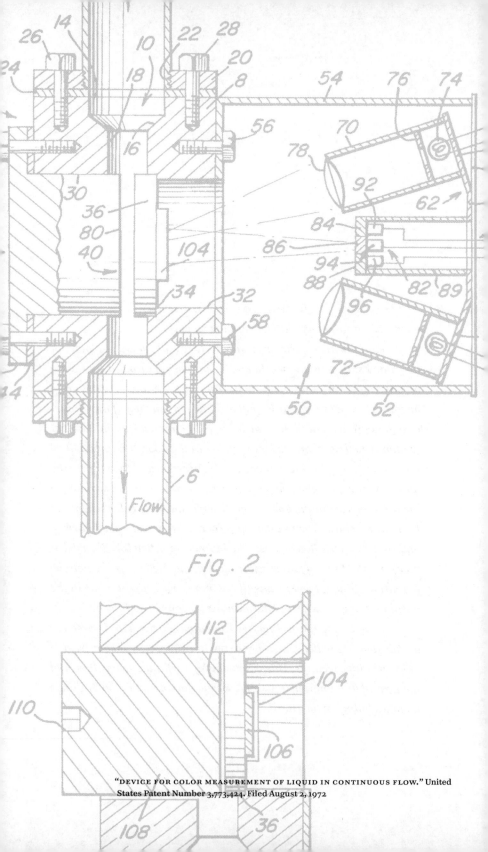

Fig. 2

"DEVICE FOR COLOR MEASUREMENT OF LIQUID IN CONTINUOUS FLOW." United States Patent Number 3,773,424. Filed August 2, 1972

XV.
Old Bill
Bethel, Connecticut, 1979–1980

LIVING WITH YOUR PARENTS AT TWENTY-THREE HAS advantages and disadvantages.

Advantages: material comfort and security, home-cooked meals, and the companionship, warmth, and understanding of those responsible for your birth and upbringing and who love – or, anyway, tolerate – you more than anyone else in the world.

Disadvantage: wanting to kill yourself.

You viewed your return home as a defeat, a humiliation, a failure. You had failed. The prodigal child home with tail between legs. Like many a prodigal child you resented your parents for this, as if they were to blame. You had yet to realize the scarcity of having these two people both together in your life, how brief their tenure would appear to you to have been when all was said and done in the big picture of your life.

Meanwhile you couldn't bear your mother's perpetual synthesis of distrust and solicitude, her legion mispronunciations and malapropisms, her hoarding economy-sized jars of mayonnaise in bulk, bouillon cubes, and Saran Wrap. Above all, you resented her for being stronger, grittier, and more self-possessed than you, her son.

Then there were your mother's migraines. They kept her bedridden for days, dry-retching into a Tupperware bowl. The migraines usually occurred on the heels of her arguments with your father, fights that often ended (as the ones between you and your brother often did) with a projectile of some kind being hurled, the hurler being your mother, the projectile an ashtray, the target a mirror that, the following day, your father would replace.

As for your father, the charming, sad, eccentric old man who wrote you all those letters, few things in life upset you more than the sight of him eating his morning toast. He would sit there, in the breakfast nook with his two three-minute eggs (one in its cup, the other on the plate next to it by his spoon) and his cup of tea (Lipton) steeping and two slices of bread (Thomas's Protein) in the toaster (burned, burning, or about to burn, as suggested by the conical umber stain on the white cabinet above the toaster), with a jar of Chivers Coarse-Cut Olde English marmalade close at hand.

Before you even entered the kitchen you'd be assailed by the acrid odor of burned toast and hear the butter knife scraping against the charred bread, followed by crunching, gurgling, and swallowing noises as your father spread more marmalade over more toast between more sips of tea, the tea-soaked but still brittle toast crashing against his dental bridgework, with crumbs of toast (not including those you would encounter later in the plumb-colored sink and clinging to the mirror of the medicine cabinet in your father's–the downstairs–bathroom) flying every which way.

Why your father's breakfast habits aggravated you so much you couldn't, and I still can't, say, but they did. They annoyed you in the extreme, to where you could no longer stomach the smell of burned toast.

Perhaps they stood for something greater than toast and tea. Maybe they were your own failings and inadequacies magnified and projected. Maybe the scorched crumbs on your father's breakfast table stood for the charred cinders of your gutted life.

YOU WERE ONLY twenty-three, yet you felt both ancient and unborn. In the mirror of your father's medicine cabinet (flecked with bits of food matter from him flossing his teeth) you studied the lines in your face–there were one or two now–as if studying the lines on one of the service station roadmaps your papa kept in the glove compartment of his Simca (and that he rarely consulted), searching for signs, shortcuts, directions.

When not sketching or writing in your basement room or floating around Bethel like a microbe, you tried to make yourself useful. One day, while your mother was in bed recovering from one of her migraines, you decided to put the house in order. You spent the morning trimming shrubs and cleaning gutters and the afternoon vacuuming, mopping, and doing laundry. With those things accomplished, you turned your attention to your mother's stove – the black antique Chamber's stove with chrome knobs that was your mother's pride and joy. You decided to clean it for her. For this task you solicited your father's help. You put him in charge of the top burners while you cleaned the oven. You handed him the can of Easy Off and went to work.

A half hour later your father called to you. You turned to see him holding two of the stove irons. They dangled from his rubber-gloved hands, dripping brownish goo on the floor and into the dog's dish as he stood there with a lost helpless look on his face.

I'm sorry, he said, but I can't seem to put this bloody thing back together. It's simply not *possible!*

You turned to the sink where he'd been washing the irons. It looked as if someone had struck oil. The counter, the curtains, the dish rack, the sponges, the potted plants – all were laced, flecked, or splattered with black grunge.

As your father continued to stand there holding the dripping irons the dog leaped up and started lapping at them.

YOU HAD JUST dropped your mother off at the hospital to have some testing done for her migraines when you saw the man in the wheelchair, the same man you had seen at the teacher's carriage house in eighth grade. You recognized the pink-orange complexion that covered half his face and the dead crow of a toupee on his head.

He was being pushed in his wheelchair to a van parked in the hospital parking lot. Though like the other it said ETTELUBMA POT-PIT across its back doors, this van was white, not red.

The attendant was a different person, too, not a black man this time but a white man with stiff white hair. Having loaded his human cargo into the back of the van he climbed into the front.

From the driver's seat of your mother's Rambler American you watched, your MG having bitten the dust.

Under gray skies you followed the van out of the hospital parking lot and through an industrial park to the interstate entrance where it climbed up the northbound ramp toward Newtown. You felt like a TV detective following it.

After a dozen miles the van exited onto a road that wound past the brick buildings of the Southbury Training School, a facility for mentally disadvantaged children.

It started raining. The van's signal lights winked as it turned onto the road to Lake Lillinonah. The lake was a fabled make-out destination for teenagers, who would park along its shore and, under cover of smooth alder and spiceberry bushes, engage in wanton acts. Along this iniquitous stretch of road the van splashed through deep puddles to a straightaway squirming with frogs, hundreds of them, their squashed bodies turning the roadway into a slimy bubbling stew.

As they rolled over the amphibious carpet, the Rambler's tires made horrible squishing sounds. An occasional torn frog specimen, tossed up by the ambulette's rear wheels, hurled itself into the Rambler's by then opaque windshield, where the dimwitted windshield wipers beat them into a relish-like consistency. You squirted blue wiper fluid, turning the mixture a muddy shade of turquoise.

Unable to see, you pulled over and, with the sleeve of your denim jacket, wiped the gooey mess away as best you could. By then your head pounded with the headache that had budded as you rose that morning and that now burst into full bloom.

On your way back to the car, your sneakers crushed more frogs, their peeps so loud you couldn't have heard yourself over them had you screamed, as you were tempted to. By the time you put the car in gear, the ambulette had vanished into the rainy night.

Still you kept driving.

Then you saw the van parked in the driveway of one of those houses they move on trucks, a double-wide, with a wooden ramp stretching from the driveway over a weedy overgrown yard to the front door.

You crept past, watching as the attendant slid the van's side door open. Holding a large tutti-frutti-colored umbrella over both their heads, he lowered his passenger to the ground, then rolled him up the ramp to the front door. The scene held you so enthralled you nearly drove into a telephone pole.

At the next driveway you turned and doubled back. That's when you saw the mailbox on the side of the road across the street from the house, with the teacher's last name spelled out in reflective stickers. You passed one more driveway before pulling over.

By then your headache throbbed. You opened the mailbox and took out all the letters inside. Mixed in with bills, circulars, and junk mail was a letter from the teacher. Postmarked Corvallis, Oregon.

You reminded yourself that stealing letters out of people's mailboxes was a federal offense. You'd be a criminal, a felon. You could go to jail.

You slid the letter into the pocket of your jean jacket, replaced the rest of the mail in the mailbox, got in the Rambler, and drove off.

* * *

THE DAY BEFORE YOU SET OFF ON YOUR WESTWARD journey, as you and your father were leaving the bank where you'd gone to purchase traveler's checks, apropos some remark you made, some grandiose ambition you'd given voice to, he said to you, *Do you know what I think, Peter, my boy? I think that you're overdrawn. Overdrawn – do you know what I mean by that?* It was one of the very few pieces of advice that your father had ever given to you, along with *Don't spend your life among machines; Never give gasoline to a slow engine;* and *Always rinse your mouth out with water before you go to bed.*

That same evening, you were sitting in a bar called the Mad Hatter's Lounge, scribbling away in your notebook when an old guy in a baseball cap stepped up to you.

Man, will you look at that hand go, he remarked with his hand on your back. Hell, I can't even think that fast. And a south-paw to boot!

The man's thin eyes gleamed; his suntanned face was leathery as a catcher's mitt. He asked if you were *a writer or something.*

Unless you want to be bugged a bar is no place to write. Knowing this, at some level you must have wanted the attention, but not from some old guy with gin-soaked eyes and a leathery face. Hoping it would make him go away you said:

I'm no writer; I'm just a bum.

It was the wrong thing to say. The man's eyes burst with indignation.

Did I just hear you right? A *bum,* is *that* what you just said?

He laid into you then, this old man you'd never in your life seen before.

A bum! Why of all the –! How dare you even *think* let alone say such a thing like that about yourself, a guy with talent like you! Talent – that's what you've got. I wish I had talent like that! A bum, you say! He shook his head. Don't you ever, ever again in your life talk that way about yourself in front of Old Bill. I *mean* it!

He grabbed your wrist, held it to his leathery cheek, and made you swear after him:

Swear to Old Bill you're no bum. *Swear it!*

I'm no bum, you swore.

You got talent. Say it!

I've got talent.

You're a winner!

I'm a winner.

You're gonna make it!

I'm gonna make it.

Never give up!

Never give up.

That's the spirit!

Old Bill slapped you hard on the back, gave your shoulder a squeeze, and left The Mad Hatter's Lounge.

IN ALBUQUERQUE YOU slept under the stars. With a guy who picked you up in his red vintage Studebaker pickup truck you spent the next six days cleaning storm-ravaged yards. At sunset after working all day you would hike up into the mountains to soak in a carbonated spring. One night you stepped out of the spring into a nest of fire ants.

East of Ash Fork a pickup truck carrying paperless day workers drove you twenty miles off course before the driver, hearing your screams, dropped you off.

In a café on Telegraph Avenue you met Darla who might have let you kiss her and maybe do more had you not been so foolish as to ask first. She suggested that you hitch your next ride on the Golden Gate Bridge.

That way, she said, if nobody stops you can always jump.

Less than three miles north of Cloverdale, California, you cursed the Winnebagos streaking by in the rain. You took refuge in a motel bar, where, with the help of your nineteen-cent Bic ballpoint pen, your wisdom teeth broke through the gums. To numb the pain and wash the blood down, the barmaid gave you a free shot of well brandy.

You were nursing the brandy and your gums when a man about your age with dirty fingernails walked in out of the rain with his bulldog-faced companion. The companion kept saying, *I mean it, Jamie, I ain't kiddin', I'm gonna leave right now, I swear to god you better come on or I'm goin' on without you.*

After the bulldog left, Jamie took out a wallet photo of his three-year-old daughter and told you how after he got his wife pregnant her dad gave him five hundred dollars for an abortion. *I took the five-hunnerd, bought me some coke and Thai stick and with the leftover twenty-five got us married in a Vegas motel.*

As Jamie said this, a flood of fresh blood gushed from your gums into your mouth. You went to the bathroom to spit it out.

Two brandy shots later you decided to pitch a tent in the Redwood National Forest. While Jamie stole some firewood from the motel porch, you made out with the barmaid in the drizzly motel parking lot.

By the time you got to the redwood forest the fog was so thick you couldn't see the gigantic trees. You got a fire started in time for the rain to whoosh down again. When it soaked through your ponchos you ditched it into a nearby latrine.

Curled up and soaked on the concrete floor, the gums of your wisdom teeth (which so far had shed only blood, no wisdom) aching, you dreamed you were a millionaire in a Hugh Hefner-style smoking jacket, giving sightseers a tour of your redwood mansion. You were deep into this dream when a female voice said, *Beg your pardon.* You opened one eye to a woman stepping over you on her way to a stall.

BACK ON THE highway, standing there alone with your thumb out, you recalled your father's words as you'd stepped out of the bank that day. *I think you're overdrawn. Do you know what I mean by that?*

It struck you that Old Bill's words had been the antithesis of your father's.

You stood there for an hour before giving up and walking two and a half miles to the nearest rest stop. While they emptied their septic tanks, you begged the Winnebago drivers for a ride to Eureka. *Please,* you said to them. *I'll give you my driver's license, you can have my wallet, I'll give you my guitar, just get me out of here!*

At last a driver had you hop in the back of a truck he was towing. You got out your guitar and strummed it with the wind whipping your hair.

In Eureka you boarded a Greyhound bound for parts north. You sat next to a heavyset Native American who'd been a professional forest fire fighter. Thanks to the smoke he'd inhaled he wheezed whenever he laughed. Meanwhile a tall, thin, shoeless, homeless man named Joe swayed in the bus aisle, bragging to anyone who'd listen that he had been in and out of jail a dozen times for tax evasion. Shoeless Joe harassed every passenger on the bus, especially the rasping fat Indian.

Shoeless Joe: *Say there, Chief Broom, where'd you get all that beefsteak?*

Fat Indian: *Hwee, Hwee, hwee.*

Shoeless Joe: *Lemme ask you something, there, Sitting Bull. What do you do when all that forest fire smoke blows your way?*

Fat Indian: *Duck! Hwee, hwee –*

Shoeless Joe: *And if you can't duck, Chief Beefsteak, whatddya do then, huh?*

Fat Indian: *Breathe it! Hwee, hwee –*

Shoeless Joe: *Can't all that smoke kill you?*

Fat Indian: *Yup! Hwee, hwee, hwee – …*

In the darkness of the rumbling bus, you wept. Precisely why you cried you weren't sure. Anyway you weren't in a position to say.

But I am. You cried because you were lost. You cried because you were confused. You cried because at twenty-three you no longer had any idea who you were.

The fat Indian, aware of your tears, hugged you without a word.

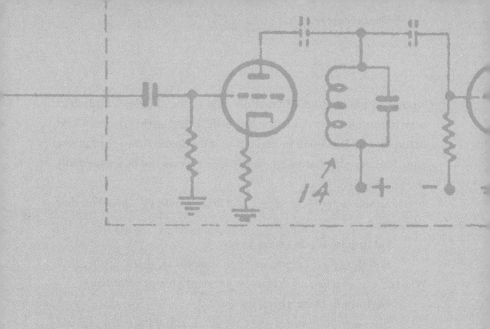

From Patent Number 2,964,641: "A graph showing a typical group of recognition signals produced when an engraving is identified."

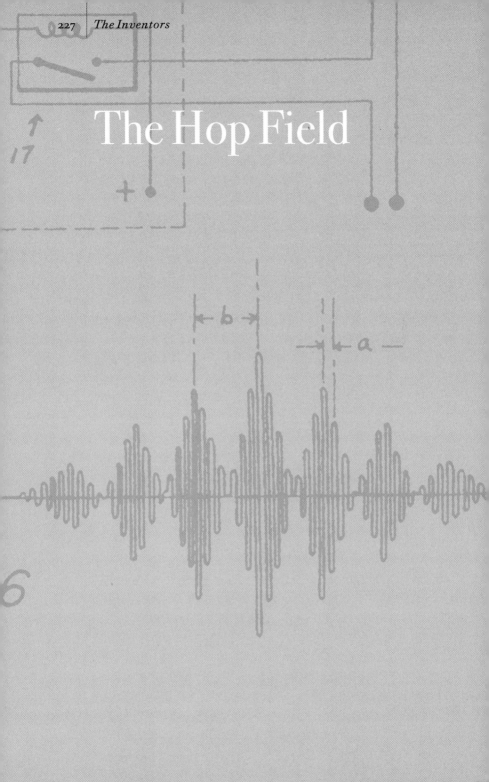

The Hop Field

INVENTOR

PAUL J.SELGIN

SINCE MOVING HERE, A GOAL OF MINE HAS BEEN TO SWIM *all year long without a wetsuit. It's warm enough here to do that. This past winter the temperature of the lake dropped no lower than 51° F. One can train oneself to swim in temperatures lower than that.*

Lynne Cox has done so. Cox is an American long-distance open water swimmer and author. She has twice broken the record for crossing the English Channel: nine hours and fifty-seven minutes in 1972, and nine hours and thirty-six minutes in 1973. She has also swum the Bering Straight, from Little Diomede Island in Alaska to Big Diomede Island in what at the time (1987) was still the Soviet Union. To this day scientists are still not sure how she was able to do it, with no wetsuit and the average temperature between 44° and 43°. A few years later she swam for over a mile in the waters of Antarctica.

My ambitions are far humbler, the difference between 44° and 50° being that between discomfort (and a good deal of shivering) and possible death by hypothermia. Two things I have learned, though: first, that there is nothing more invigorating and healthful than swimming in cold water, the colder the better, up to a point; second, that much of what we experience as discomfort in cold water comes down to attitude. How we approach the water matters. If you say to yourself, "By God – I'm going to freeze!" you will probably experience something like that. On the other hand, if as you ease yourself into the water with the equivalent of an orgasmic sigh, saying to yourself, "This is nothing – really nothing; it's not really that cold at all," you will discover to your surprise that it's just so – not that cold at all. By the time you've swum ten strokes, you'll be convinced. It works. Try it.

It's the same with writing – especially with writing a book. I tell my students this. You have to go in slowly and talk yourself out of any fear. Or just take a plunge – don't give a shit. (Jump, Papa, Jump!) But whatever you do, don't sit there dwelling on how cold the water is.

* * *

MORNING NOW. THE SKY OVERCAST, THE AIR GRAY. A bird sings. Yesterday I had a tree expert out here to look at a big white pine near the dock that has shed half its needles. As I suspected, the tree is dead, a victim of the bark beetles that have attacked and killed so many pines here and elsewhere. There is nothing for it; it has to come down, and the sooner the better, before the beetles go from it to the next.

The tree is at least seventy-five feet tall. He quoted me $1,000 for the job. I'm no good at bargaining with contractors. Instead of saying, "That seems pretty steep. Sure you can't do me any better?" my first impulse is to be agreeable. So I agreed. Only later did my neighbor tell me he paid just $1,200 to have three equally tall pine trees removed. At least it will be done quickly – this Tuesday. With luck the other pines will be spared.

But probably not. The same neighbor told me, "With pine trees you have two choices. Take 'em all down at once, or watch 'em come down one by one." The principle here being (if I understood my neighbor correctly) that if something's bound to die sooner or later, let it die sooner.

Not a principle I care to apply to too many things. Certainly not to my own life, or to these memories that, like my poor pine tree, have the equivalent of bark beetles gnawing at them.

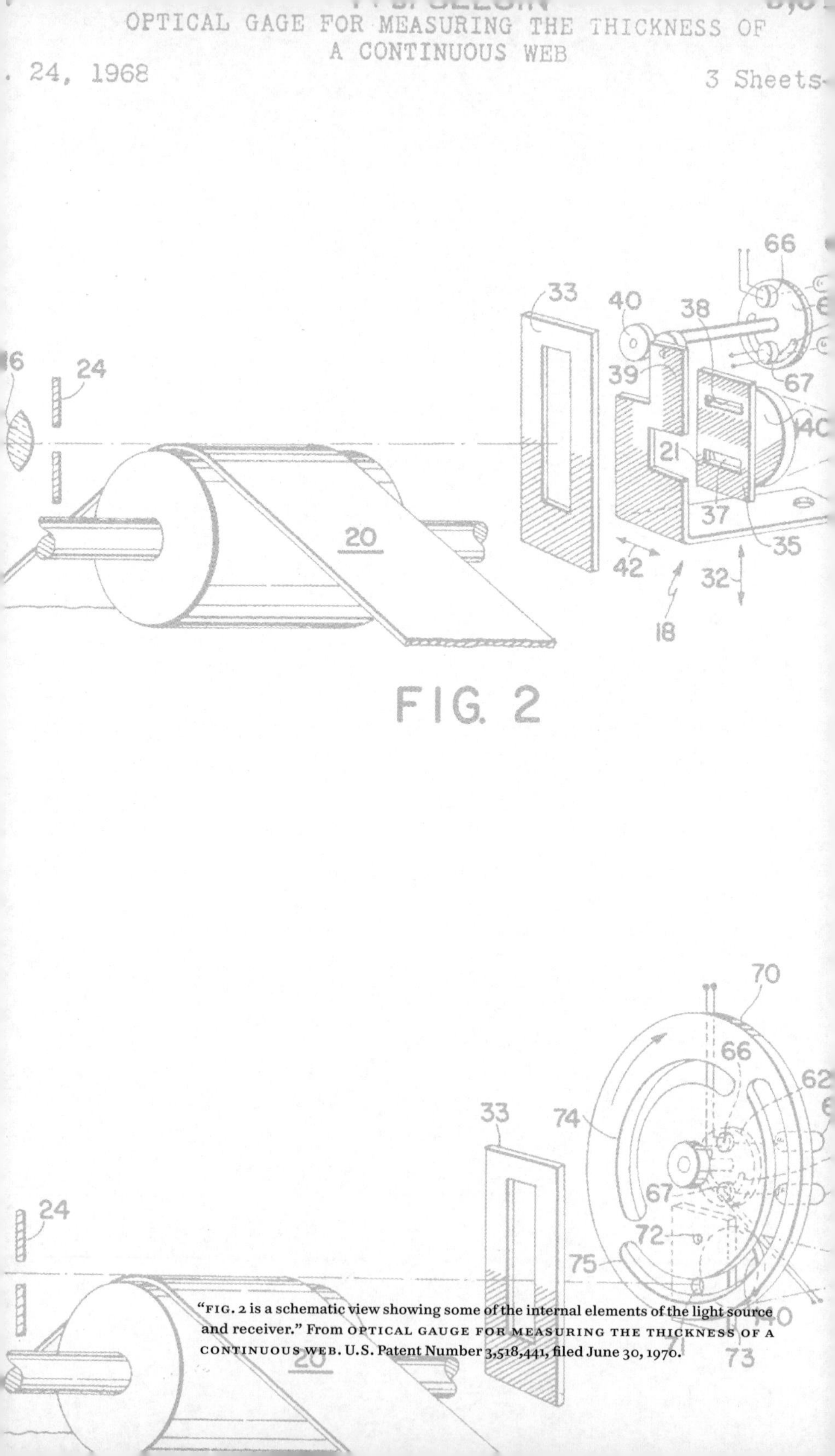

FIG. 2

"FIG. 2 is a schematic view showing some of the internal elements of the light source and receiver." From OPTICAL GAUGE FOR MEASURING THE THICKNESS OF A CONTINUOUS WEB. U.S. Patent Number 3,518,441, filed June 30, 1970.

XVI.
Corvallis, Oregon, 1980

YOU'RE LYING IN A HOP FIELD. IT'S TWO A.M. THE SKY is dark, the surrounding mountains darker. You look at the stars, trying to name the constellations. You think you see Orion's Belt, but you're not sure. Twenty-three years old and you still don't have the constellations down.

The year is 1980. The hop field is in Corvallis, Oregon, population 30,000, a town of farmers, students, and aging hippies eighty miles south of Portland. The name derives from the Latin *cor vallis*, or "corn valley."

You arrived here two hours ago with your guitar, a notebook, and a folder full of letters, having hitchhiked across the country to see your former eighth-grade English teacher, a two-week journey that began with you standing with your thumb out on a freeway ramp in Connecticut and ended when the gloomy bus dropped you off at the edge of town, five miles from here.

* * *

AT FIRST CORVALLIS LOOKED LIKE ANY SMALL TOWN after nightfall. Stores and buildings hunkered under a half moon, ice cream parlor, drug store, a movie theater showing an Indiana Jones caper. It might have been Bethel, your own hometown, save for the smell of coffee suffusing the moonlit air.

In the shadow of the bus depot you adjusted your backpack. Four of your fingers had blood blisters from carrying your guitar case. You took a folded badly battered envelope from your back pocket. By the light of a streetlamp, as if you hadn't long since committed it to memory, you studied the return address: 65 Goodnight Avenue.

You started walking.

Two dozen yards later a set of twirling red and blue lights blinded you. The cruiser pulled over. The cop pointed his flashlight in your face. He asked you for your ID. You produced your Connecticut driver's license. He asked what you were doing in Corvallis at midnight. You told him you were there to see a friend. *What's your friend's name?*

As you answered, you were reminded of a similar incident ten years earlier back in Bethel, when that policeman pulled you and the teacher over and interrogated you, how the teacher told him (not in so few words) to fuck off. You remembered how impressed you'd been by that, how cool it seemed to you, how the cop cursed, spit a tawny projectile of tobacco juice, laid rubber, and took off. You considered saying something of the sort to this concerned, dutiful enforcer of the law. But you were too exhausted, too brittle, too anxious to get where you were going to pull a stunt like that.

Are you aware, the cop said (holding his big flashlight by the neck with three fingers, like a doctor holding a stethoscope, its beam still blinding you) that it is illegal to stand off the curb in the state of Oregon? Disorderly conduct. I could arrest you. Are you aware of that?

Nossir, you said. I was not aware of that.

Since you're from out of state I'll let you go with just a warning this time.

The cop lowered the flashlight.

Now please step back onto the sidewalk. Long as you're on the sidewalk you may hitchhike legally in the state of Oregon.

He was about to drive off when you asked for directions to Goodnight Avenue.

Five miles straight ahead to your left.

You thanked him.

Just stay on the curb, said the police officer.

IN THE SKY over a river the moon glowed. You shivered. Buildings turned to houses, then into fields. Off the macadam compounded with mica moonlight glittered. The mellow coffee smell was replaced by an acrid odor of fertilizer. A plane's red anti-collision light flashed through the darkness.

You'd walked for over an hour when you saw the street sign rising black against the night sky. Goodnight Avenue. A half mile down the road you found the mailbox. 65. On the same side of the road, a field so bright with moonlight it looked like an ocean. On the other side, the silhouette of a one-story house.

A light burned in one of the windows.

You picked up your guitar and stepped toward the house. As you did, the tension mounted in your shoulders and neck. Your tongue and mouth went dry as if coated with dust. Your breath quivered.

YOU WERE SHAKING all over.

At the front door you stood, hearing your heart race, thinking *nothing has changed.* Ten years have passed but I'm still thirteen, you thought, still standing across the street from the teacher's front door, wondering what to do. Still as naive and needy as ever.

And what did you have to show for all those years? Had you saved any lives, led any uprisings, fought any wars? You'd filled a bunch of notebooks with sketches and scribbles, learned to play the guitar, written a few songs. Fiddling while Rome burns. *Do any of us really self-actualize?* The teacher's pet, his prize pupil.

Now look at you.

You turned, re-crossed the road, and kept walking, into the hop field, the one you're lying in now, gazing up at the sky powdered with stars, trying to pick out the constellations. Among the stars, one star stands out, brighter than all the others. You reach for it with your eyes. With your eyes still reaching you fall asleep.

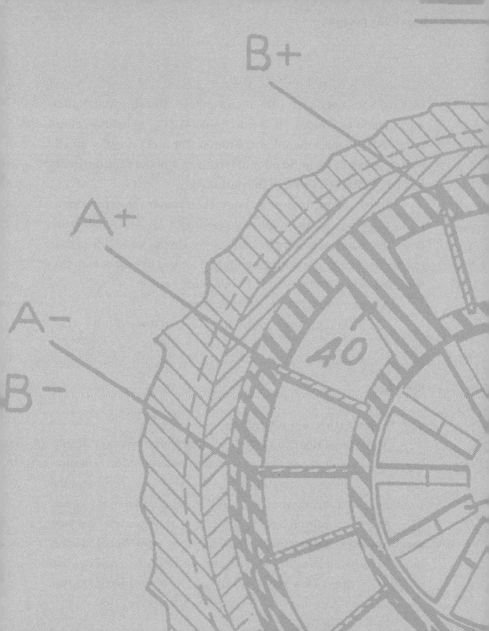

B+

A+

A−

B−

40

From U.S. Patent No. 4,218,525, filed Sept. 21, 1949 for RESERVE TYPE BATTERY, "a reserve battery comprising a cell, spaced electrodes in said cell, a filling aperture in said cell, a frangible sealed ampule containing electrolyte, a plunger adjacent said ampule, a conduit between said ampule and said cell aperture, a body of sealing material, and means for moving said plunger into contact with said ampule to crush same and force electrolyte through said conduit and aperture into said cell, said means being so constructed and arranged that upon further motion of said plunger the body of sealing material is disposed across the aperture to seal same." The illustration ("FIG. 2") is "a cross-section view taken on line 2-2 of FIG. 1."

Controlled Burn

TODAY THE WRITING GOES SLOWLY. JUST GETTING WORDS on paper feels awkward and strange, like the timid first steps of a recovering stroke victim. Two weeks ago, while tending his yard, my neighbor two houses down, a man named Mitch in his mid-sixties, suffered a stroke that left him paralyzed on his left side. I saw him yesterday sitting in the passenger seat of a red SUV that had pulled up to his mailbox. I had been raking leaves. I'd assumed he was still in the hospital. I dropped the rake and ran over. His son was at the wheel and Virginia, his wife, in the backseat. He was trying to take the mail out of the box, struggling. Letters in various-sized envelopes trembled in his grip. It took all his will to keep from dropping them all and failing at this undertaking, which, two weeks earlier, would not even have earned that designation. Still, under the pale baseball cap and behind the large aviator-style glasses he wears, he looked chipper.

"How are you?" I said. Mitch nodded and smiled. That's when I realized he couldn't speak. In the backseat Virginia answered for him: "He's doing fine."

Just as a few days ago Mitch wouldn't have thought twice about collecting his mail, there was a time not so long ago when I wouldn't have thought twice about turning my thoughts into words in this notebook. I would have approached that task (again, if it could be called that) with as little fear as I'd approach any humble chore, washing dishes or raking leaves. I recall (with a blush of embarrassment) the letters I used to write regularly to friends, long ones into which I poured whatever came to me: idle descriptions, thoughts, ideas, feelings, hopes, worries, plans, bits of novels and stories, word-sketches of paintings in progress, I'd just write and write – or type, rather, since back then I still used a typewriter, my Remington "Noiseless" that weighed thirty-five pounds and, with two fingers snapping out sixty-five words per minute, sounded like a machine gun. It didn't matter what I wrote, just as long as I filled pages. When I'd filled enough pages to challenge the limitations of a first-class postage stamp, I'd sign the last page, shove the sheaf into an envelope, and send the letter off. It never even occurred to me that I might bore the pants off my correspondent. I was baring and sharing my soul, that's how I saw it, giving what I had to give. Between friends, what could possibly be wrong with that? How could they fail to be touched by my uninhibited outpourings – my essence excreted in typewritten words on paper? I had no idea then that I was honoring a great Japanese literary convention, following the brush, practicing flow: writing zuihitsu.

I want to be known; I want to understand myself and be understood. There seems to be some shame connected with this, some tacit agreement among humans that the baring of souls in the form of the written word is disagreeable, that if it must be done at all it should be done discretely, as "literature," under the guise of poetry or fiction, and not – unless the author can claim victimhood or fame – in the form of a memoir. Public and private selves are to be kept distinct.

To that I say, "pooh!"

Here is where I've come from, who I've been, what I was. What you, dear Past Self, underwent on the way to becoming me.

XXIII
Values & Proportions
Bethel, Connecticut, 1996

YOU SEE ... THE PROPORTION ...

Your father blinks his light-gray eyes, massages a perturbed brow. Propped in his rocking chair, an unspecified mass, his brain a set of crossed wires, a shorted circuit.

You ask him if he knows who you are.

Oh yes. There's a value. A little bit higher, maybe. Yes I would say that there is a positive value. Higher than most.

Do you know my name, Papa? Can you say it?

Well, yes, in a sense. Yes. That is, I know the value, the proportion....

It all comes down to proportions and values, plus and minus; high or low. If he can just assign the proper values, things will sort themselves out, the hidden properties will reveal themselves. If he could decide, for instance, what value to assign to the particular essence that is you, his son (though he recognizes neither *you* nor his *son*)... if he could assume, for instance, that your assigned value is plus or minus eight, then things would be all right; everything would be fine.

Let's try it, he says, holding your hand, straining as he grips it – no longer simply or just "your hand" but an integral part of the all-encompassing universe. *All right,* he says. *Let's do it, then; let's assign it a value. A coefficient.*

All right, you say.

Right. Go ahead, then. Do it.

The fingers of your other hand polish the rocking chair's wooden arm.

So, he says, tensing, turning red. *Fine. Come on. Let's do it …*

* * *

HE WAS SHOPPING FOR A PAIR OF SNEAKERS WHEN THE stroke occurred. The parking lot of the Thom McAn store. A cloudy day. They had left the store and were walking through the parking lot when, a few yards from your mother's Rambler, he froze. She called to him – *Paolo?* Your father stared off into space.

You were vacationing with your wife in New Jersey when you got the news. You'd been married for four years. Paulette. Petite former dancer. High cheekbones, curly hair. Like you she had Italian roots. Sicilian. True to your father, you held no trace of nationalism. Still, you took comfort in her fondness for anchovies and espresso.

So far your marriage had been good. For thirteen more years it would stay that way. You were both successful, earning livings in ways that, if not direct expressions of your art, related to it. She produced and wrote children's television shows, you did corporate caricatures and editorial illustration. You owned your first apartment, a two-bedroom deco job on the Upper West Side. Having no children or plans for any, you could afford trips to Europe – Italy, usually – every few years. Otherwise you vacationed closer to home. That summer, you rented the cottage on Lake Kinnelawn, forty minutes from the city in New Jersey. You swam and sailed a twelve-foot dingy. Paulette read mystery novels and cooked.

The last time you and your father had seen each other you argued. He said his back was bothering him. You suggested that his sneakers might be to blame, that he get himself a decent pair of new ones to replace the Goodwill tennis shoes he favored.

What do sneakers have to do with my bloody back? your father argued.

The discussion took place in the rebuilt Building, the original having burned down five years earlier when a carpet installer your father rented storage space to (and who'd been sleeping there at night after separating from his wife) left a kerosene heater burning. Building #2 had bright white linoleum-tiled floors. No more rotting holes. No mice or spiders or snakes. Most of the machinery and tools had to be replaced. Gone were most of your father's paintings and notebooks, destroyed by the fire or by the water an inept volunteer fire department pumped lavishly on it. Gone too was the original Building's smell, that special blend of scorched metal shavings, orange rind, solder smoke, and your father's frequent farts. The two lathes and his typewriter survived.

Since the fire your father had changed, too. He'd grown older, sadder, slower. His gray eyes had lost their intent gleam. He no longer smiled when working. His face was a flaccid mask of preoccupied abstraction. For this and other reasons you checked your fury at his contempt for your suggestions.

Those tennis shoes you're wearing don't have enough arch support, Papa. They're okay for playing tennis, but not for standing and working all day like you do.

Ach, don't be ridiculous! (said with that familiar dismissive wave).

It's true. You need decent arch support. No wonder your back is bugging you. Ask a doctor if you won't believe me.

Ach!

That in general your father refused to take your suggestions seriously frustrated and at times infuriated you. It wasn't just his refusal to be persuaded that frustrated you, but his way of refusing, the scorn that accompanied his dismissive gestures, his *achs* and his *aughhs*. That, not his lack of paternal pride, is what made you so angry with your father at times. That he'd directed the same scorn toward his mother, your mother, your brother, creamers that didn't pour properly, televangelists, and the country of his birth, didn't in the least mitigate your frustration or lessen your anger.

Fine, you said at last. Do whatever the hell you want. It's *your* bloody back.

A week later your mother phoned you to tell you about the stroke. You left Paulette at Lake Kinnelawn and rode a series of trains to Connecticut. On the journey's final leg, from the worn baize seat of the dilapidated Budd car you watched a litter-strewn summer landscape slide by. You'd taken this journey so frequently every last patch of sooty ballast and grimy weed was ingrained in your senses. It felt as if that train were taking you back through time, as though the rundown Budd car were bound not for Bethel, Connecticut, but for your childhood, that largely imaginary realm of joyful anticipation.

                    * * *

YOUR MOTHER MET YOU AT THE DEPOT. NORMALLY YOUR father would have been there to pick you up, standing by his latest rusting late-model European car, smiling, waving his lint-flecked beret over his thin gray head. In decades of greeting you at train stations he always looked the same. *Ah, Peter, Peter my boy!* he'd say, clasping and patting you on the back. Even through layers of winter clothes, you'd smell the dander and musk that clung to him always, the smell of the terrycloth robe in his plum-colored bathroom.

   Now your mother hugs you. In place of your father's smell there's the waxy odor of lipstick. She's had her hair colored and teased. Your mother is always having things done to her hair. She is fiercely devoted, in descending order, to her children, her good looks, and her anxieties. She lives in a fortress of anxiety, its closets jammed with solvents, unguents, pastes, and powders meant to eradicate her distress. At times she is as remote and exotic to you as Tripoli, her birthplace, with its date palms and slender minarets. Still she's your mother and you are damned if you don't love her.

   How is he doing? you ask.

   Your mother shakes her head. She's frightened, you can tell. So are you.

   Dey did more tess dis morning, she says. Dey tink maybe is someting to do wid hees blood. After lunch we go see him.

YOUR MOTHER DRIVES you home. It's been a while since you've seen the house. Not only has it fallen into disrepair, it seems diminished. Growing up there you had the impression of enormous wealth: the endlessly long driveway framed by elephantine weeping willows, the Cape Cod with its fancy brick facade and gaily striped awnings over its dormer windows, the Building with its array of mysterious outlying structures, the picket fence running up the hill to meet the mulberry tree growing in the corner of the yard, the perfectly round hedges, the stone terraces climbing into the woods, the woods themselves, with their own treasures of moss, lichen, ferns, rocks, crevices, and caves, yours all the way to the summit, from which you could see most of the town.

Now most of the willows have fallen. With its missing tines the picket fence looks like a bum's rotten teeth, its once gleaming whitewash turned to dust. Where not overgrown, the lawn is scorched brown. Flowerbeds have gone to seed. Errant shoots sprout from the hedges. Bent scraps of siding cling to the house, one gutter dangles, the others are packed with mulch. The white birch in the turnaround has devolved into a toadstool-festooned stump. From the terraced garden walls, chunks of concrete have gone missing. Dead leaves everywhere. Your father's car not in its usual spot.

Things aren't much better inside. A smell of mildew hangs everywhere. The walls need paint. The furnishings you once considered fit for a king now look bedraggled and small, the sad detritus of a petite-bourgeois existence. As for your father's paintings of which you were once so proud, and which for you were of a piece with the greatest van Goghs and Matisses, you now see them for what they really are: the slapdash dabblings of gifted amateur, their brushstrokes haphazard, their colors muddy, their materials and frames equally shoddy. How the Selgins had come down in the world!

LUNCH: DEVILED EGGS, *insalata russa, peperonata.* All your favorites. As your mother and you sit eating across from each other at the glass-topped kitchen table, your mother suddenly weeps.

I sorry, she says, reaching for and taking your hand. Forgive me.

What's the matter? Why are you crying?

I never mean to hurt you papa.

What are you talking about? you ask, though you have a pretty good idea. Mr. Peck, the "friend of the family" who lives among birch trees on an isolated hill, whose protruding lower lip glistens with spittle, who voted for Goldwater, who owns rental properties including a small motel and a factory that makes wooden boxes, but never spends his money, who (unlike your father) fought in World War II. On landing at Normandy as bullets zinged past him, he who never learned to swim said *Hallelujah*. Having resisted them for years, your mother had finally given in to his advances and let herself have an affair with him – her first and only. By then your father had already had many.

I should never have go with him, says your mother tearfully.

Why did you?

I fell sorry for him. Ee was lonely.

When your father suffered the first of his strokes, Mr. Peck advised your mother to divorce him. When she refused, he launched a tirade, telling her what a lazy, cowardly, selfish, arrogant, unpleasant, egocentric man she had married. When she defended your father, Mr. Peck became abusive, mocking her, calling her a damned fool, a martyr, his spittle flying from his lower lip until she ran from his shingled house.

I say to myself I never going back!

But a few days later your mother found herself and her Rambler parked once again in the driveway of Mr. Peck's cedar shingled house.

It took a car accident to end the affair. They were coming home from an overnight trip to see the fall colors in Vermont when the brakes on Mr. Peck's Plymouth (which, being too parsimonious for service stations, he repaired himself) failed and they collided with a highway department sand truck. They returned from the hospital in matching neck braces. Mr. Peck insisted that the accident hadn't been his fault, that the driver of the sand truck had run his stop sign, when in fact he had done so. Rather than have her file a claim with his insurance company, he tried to get your mother to let him pay her hospital bill. She filed a claim. She also sued him, and won.

Since then, she and Mr. Peck had not spoken to each other.

* * *

AS YOU STEP INTO THE HOSPITAL ROOM, YOUR FATHER sits up, smiling, aware of your combined essences, yours and your mother's, as if a strong perfume has permeated the sterile hospital room. Despite the summer heat you've worn your new hat, a floppy newsboy cap, the sort worn by James Cagney and other movie gangsters in forties melodramas. Unable to identify you by name or relation, having no words for *hat* or *cap*, your father remarks as you stand there wearing it at a rakish tilt:

You – look – vaguely – disreputable.

His lunch tray sits untouched. Roast chicken and peas gone cold because he either cannot see or doesn't recognize them. In a too-loud voice my mother asks:

PAOLO, HOW DO YOU FEEL?

Your father thinks. That's all that's left of him: his thinking, a generalized deliberation or rumination that spreads itself across space and time like a valorous coat across a mud puddle, a weightless brooding suspended in a void, free of object or agency. Your father sees you there, but only as one sees a concept, an idea off to the side of the central topic, a vitreous floater, a shadow on the wall.

He sings:

In olden days a glimpse of stocking
Was looked on as something shocking
Now heaven knows – anything goes …

– waving one hand like conductor's baton while tapping out the rhythm with a stiff finger on his skull.

Heaven knows: anything goes …

Your mother spoon-feeds him. Mashed peas. Chocolate pudding. Later, the duty nurse helps him into a wheelchair. You roll him down the corridor to a lounge with a large plate glass window. Scudding clouds, blue sky, hills of blazing autumn trees. You describe the view, a Hudson River landscape by Thomas Cole or Frederick Church. He sees something more like Mondrian's Broadway Boogie-Woogie. *I feel the value in this instant to be quite high, I'd say at least plus or minus ... oh ... I don't know, eighteen or thereabouts.* He goes on about proportions and relative values and how it may be best to increase the coefficient by a percentage of the total variation.

You think you understand him.

True, you say. But the important thing is it's a beautiful day. *Ah yes, that is true, I suppose. Yes, that's important ...*

* * *

FROM THAT FIRST STROKE YOUR FATHER MOSTLY RECOV-ered, but other episodes followed: sudden blank looks while watching television, delayed answers to simple questions. One morning, home for another weekend visit, you heard a strained voice calling from the garage. You went out to find him there, in the backseat of the Opel he was no longer supposed to drive, saying, *Ah, there you are, Peter, old boy. Perhaps you'll enlighten me. I can't seem to find the bloody steering wheel!*

Over the next year, by invisible increments, the loss of proper names and nouns became permanent. The objects of this world were suitcases without handles; your father couldn't grasp them. His memories were next to go. One by one like unfaithful friends they deserted him.

You tried to help him remember. You'd sit with him in the living room where he'd been relegated to his rocking chair, reminding him of things, saying *this is your house* and *I'm your son, Peter* and *You have sons, twins, Peter and George. ...*

You reminded him of his inventions, of the Color Coder and the Thickness Gauge and the Blue Jean Machine. *Remember? Your lab is at the bottom of the driveway. The Building, we call it. It burned down, but you had it rebuilt. Remember? The floors used to be rotten. Mice and snakes lived there. I used to visit you down there. I'd watch you working at the lathe, the typewriter, the band saw. At the ends of*

our visits, on our way up the driveway to the house, we'd stop for a pee.
Remember? (If you could just make him remember a few things, it
would help; it would save a bit of your father for you.)

    ... *You're my father, my papa.*

    ... *I'm your son, Peter.*

    ... *You invented the first dollar-bill changing machine. The*
Nomoscope.

    ... *Remember the Nomoscope?*

For your sake and your father's you tried to remember the
good things. Exploring the beds of abandoned railways, those early
trips to New York, the Hotel Paris ...

    ... *Remember the Hotel Paris, Papa?*

Five years had passed since you and your father were last in
New York together. He visited you not long after you and Paulette
bought your apartment. It was his first trip there in years and would
be his last. The apartment was on West Ninety-fourth. He found a
parking space three blocks away on Columbus Avenue and rang the
lobby buzzer. You showed him your sunken living room that you had
decorated with paintings of the sinking *Titanic*. Then you went to a
nearby diner for lunch. Your father ordered vegetable barley soup.
When you asked him how it was, he looked at the soup spoon trem-
bling in his fist and said, in a voice leaden with sorrow, *Not so hot.*
He had come to the city to see you, true, but also to gain an audi-
ence with the literary agent to whom he had sent his latest magnum
opus, a manuscript titled *Beyond Pragmatism*, by which he hoped to
advance the theories of William James into the twenty-first century,
a futile hope for this obdurate eccentric who rarely read anything
published after the Hague Peace Conference and whose manifes-
toes were riddled with hyphenated *to-days* and plastered with Ko-
Rec-Type. The literary agent had not returned his calls.

Having paid for your disappointing lunch, he repaired to a
telephone booth across the street, where, for the eighth time so far
that day, he tried to reach the agent, only to lose a quarter to the out-
of-service payphone. You stood there and watched as with unchar-
acteristic fury he slammed the receiver down, nearly breaking it.

Three blocks away, you found another phone booth, this one occupied by a young African-American man, prompting your father, until that moment the least bigoted person you'd ever known, to combine a garden-variety epithet with a racial slur.

Papa, take it easy, you'd said – or something to that effect. What's *wrong?*

But you knew perfectly well. The city was no longer his city, the innocent one he took you to on his "business trips" when you were a child, the one he had invented for you. It had become an alien place, a hostile place. By then you knew those early "business trips" to the city with your papa hadn't been so innocent, either, that he'd kept his mistress there, or more than one mistress. You knew at least one name, Berenice *(Beh – reh – nee – chay)*, a name that would occupy roughly the same plane in your pubescent mind as the devil until that day when its owner appeared at your father's funeral wearing a reindeer-and-snowflake sweater.

As you led him away from the telephone booth, you read in your father's murky gray pupils a look of accusation and betrayal, as if you, his son – not New York City or his literary agent – had let him down. It had struck you then that at seventy-six your father was a deeply disappointed man, a man whose genius had failed him. The Color Coder, the Thickness Gauge, the Shoe Sole and Blue Jean Machines … all the patents and unpublished manuscripts, the hundreds of slapdash paintings, a lifetime's worth of inventions (most of them no longer in use): none would survive him. Along with that look of betrayal in your father's eyes that day you saw a man haunted by failure, whose supply of latent talents, however impressive, couldn't meet the demands of his ambitions, who understood that life would give him no more chances. A man who, in a word – your father's word, a word he had once applied to you – was *overdrawn.*

* * *

THAT YOUR OWN SENSE OF FAILURE WAS INEXTRICABLY bound up with your father's made his waning all the more bittersweet to you. If only you could make him see that he hadn't failed *you*, that of his dozens of inventions, you alone would survive him; that by your failing alone could he truly fail. How urgently you wanted him to know this – and how much more urgently you your-self needed to believe that you hadn't and would not fail, that the invention known as Peter Selgin would not only survive, but thrive.

Your last visit with your father before he had the first stroke did nothing to assuage your feelings of failure or your resentment. During an autumn visit – the same autumn when your mother and Mr. Peck returned from the hospital in neck braces – two months prior to your argument over sneakers, you shared with your father a short story you had written. You did so reluctantly, having by then endured his harsh criticism many times. This time, though, you had cause to be optimistic. After all, you'd worked hard. You'd published a few stories. You had reason to believe that your work was good, or at least that it wasn't terrible. From a few feet behind his rocking chair you watched your father turn a page, then anoth-er. He sighed, rubbed his forehead, shook his head, groaned, and made his disapproval known in other graphic and audible ways.

Six pages into the story, with an extra loud *arghh,* he hand-ed it back to you.

I'm sorry, he said. But I simply can't go on.

Why? What's wrong with it?

Oh, Peter, I don't know where to begin.

Come off it, Papa. It can't be *that* bad!

Oh but it is – it is!

Tell me why, at least.

You write too much for *effect*. You show off. You must learn to humble yourself. Whenever you think you've done something terribly clever, think again. (You recalled your father's criticism of Proust's metaphors.) Apart from which your punctuation and grammar leave a lot to be desired.

Though you were tempted to argue, you thought better of it and let the matter drop until later that day when you and your father went for a walk together in the woods behind the house.

You'd been walking for some time, neither of you saying a word, when out of the silence you blurted:

You never did put much stock in me, Papa, did you?

What does that mean?

You have no faith in me, that's what it means.

Ach – faith!

Yes, Papa, faith.

Are you talking about your story? Is that what this is about? Really, Peter, you take things too personally!

Maybe so. Still, it's a fact that you never really encouraged us. Me or George. Ask George. He'll tell you as much.

Ach! Just because I don't care for this latest story of yours. Of *course* I've encouraged you.

Really? When, Papa?

What?

When was the last time you encouraged me?

Oh, for the love … I can't recall a particular time. But I have. I *have!*

Your father's face had turned red. You changed the subject then, asking about the horsetail ferns that once grew along the trail where you were hiking but had vanished.

I wonder what happened to them?

Your father shook his head. It's not true, he said. I've always done my best to encourage you. Always! As for your writing, well, either it's good or it isn't. You don't want me to lie to you, do you?

No, Papa, I don't want you to lie.

Well, then …

Still, it would be nice if you could be a little more encouraging.

But how can I encourage work that *isn't good?* (The question had a pleading, desperate tone to it.)

I rest my case.

I didn't mean it that way! You know I didn't mean it that way!

Your father's face had turned red again. It was the face of a man in agony. You felt bad then. It wasn't your father's fault, after all, if your stories weren't any good, was it? Nor is there a law that says a father needs to approve of – let alone admire – the performances of his children, however dismal.

Please, you said. Don't get upset. Let's just drop it, okay? It's not important.

Which only upset your father further. Which was what you had wanted, or thought you had wanted, wasn't it: to make your poor old papa feel like shit. Now that you had achieved your goal you felt like shit yourself.

You waited for the blood to drain from your father's face, then walked silently together back to the house.

* * *

DURING YOUR FINAL VISITS WITH HIM, HIS STROKES having rendered him no longer able to care for himself, much less to work or read or write or paint or do any of the things he loved, you sometimes slept with your father. Someone had to sleep with him to make sure that he didn't fall out of the bed and bleed to death from the medicine doctors prescribed to thin his blood. You did it for your mother, to give her a break. Otherwise, she slept with him.

Now and then, your father would "soil himself." The expression amused you. You pictured a Sunday gardener in canvas shoes and straw hat stooped over a mound of soil shaped like your father, mulched, seeded, fertilized, sprouting tea roses and gardenias.

Your father smelled: the rank, cheesy odor of human decrepitude. Before climbing into bed with him you'd rub a dab of Vicks VapoRub underneath your nostrils. Then you'd tuck your father in and kiss his stubbled cheek.

Before he had his strokes, your father suffered from insomnia. Now he slept like a child. Lying with him on a convertible couch in the den that had been your grandmother's room, you slept well, too.

YOU WAKE TO *your father's growling basso profundo as he inveighs against your mother, who, with her thick accent, reasons with him, or tries to. You get up, put on your robe, and follow the sounds to their source downstairs.*

Ma Paolo, your mother says. Is only twenty dollar more a month.

Another twenty dollars, your father grumbles in English. And another twenty, and another! What do you think, that I'm made of money? (He doesn't want to spend the twenty dollars a month to insure the Building against fire.)

Ma Paolo, sii ragionevole! If someting 'appen –

Nothing's going to happen, damn it. You won't be stuck with any bills, if that's what you're worried about. I have savings. I'll pay for the bloody fire, if there is one. I'll pay for my funeral, too, if you're worried about that as well.

Paolo –

Vile, cretinous –

From the dream of your parents arguing you drift into another dream, one of you naked and smeared with shit, running through the lobby of a movie theater packed with giggling girls. The dream carries you to the summit of mortification.

Then you wake up.

THE VICKS VAPORUB has worn off. You smell a dark, deep, pungent odor. Your father whimpers. You switch on the lamp. Smeared across your father's thigh is damning evidence that he has "soiled" himself. The brown smudge mocks you. You close your eyes to ferns swaying in a breeze. With your eyes still closed, your mind drifts over Huntington Lake, to the island with the lighthouse. You feel the sun on your eyelids. The smell of excrement reasserts itself. You open your eyes to your beshitted father.

You consider appealing to your mother but don't want to wake her.

You wonder: should I clean up the bed first and then my father, or vice versa? To clean the bed I'll have to get my father out of it, which will mean sitting him in a chair. But then the chair will get "soiled." I'll have to put a towel down on it, you think. But which towel? Does my mother keep a special towel for that purpose? Would it be morally defensible to use a towel and then, without telling anyone, throw it into the hamper and let it be used again for normal purposes? Has my mother done just that? you wonder. Have I dried myself with a towel or towels that have touched my father's "soiled" flesh? Does it matter?

As your father whimpers, using an old towel from under the kitchen sink, you wipe the floppy globes of his rump, the web-like undersides of his knees, the flat white base of his spine, the sacks of exhausted muscle clinging to his upper arms. Your father's a baby and you're his mother, Nonnie. *Stronzo!* As you wipe him you look out the window at the crescent moon shining there like a fingernail paring.

Having cleaned him, you guide your father to his rocking chair and sit him down.

Don't move, you say. *Stay right there, I'll be right back. Okay?*

* * *

YOU BUNDLE UP THE SHITTY SHEETS AND CARRY THEM downstairs to the laundry room. To get there you have to pass the furnace area, where your mother makes bridal headpieces she sells on consignment at a boutique in town where she works. She keeps her sewing machine, her boxes of beads and sequins and lace, her ribbons and silk netting and crinoline, there. Like galaxies strung out across the night sky, six of her latest headpieces, a pristine row of them, hang from a length of clothesline suspended between the fuel oil tank and the furnace. The headpieces are worth seventy-five to a hundred dollars each.

As you're passing by it with the bundled sheets the furnace clicks and roars to life, startling you so you instinctively whip around with the bundle. The centrifugal force of the sudden movement splatters your father's loose bowel movement across the headpieces, strafing them with brown bullets of liquid shit.

Back upstairs, you find your father on the floor in front of his rocking chair. Your mother stands there looking awful in a rose-colored nightgown you bought her many Christmases ago.

Where were you? she asks.

Taking care of something.

What happen to de bed?

I'm taking care of it.

Together you and your mother put fresh sheets on the bed and tuck your father in. Afterward you get back into bed yourself.

BUT YOU CAN'T sleep. To the sound of the washing machine rumbling downstairs you picture your mother's headpieces being agitated along with your father's shit.

Your thoughts drift to the night the Building burned. You'd been sleeping soundly, not with your stroke-addled papa in the den that had been your grandmother's room, but alone in your basement bedroom, when the pounding on the front door woke you.

You put on your pajama bottoms, rushed upstairs, and opened the door to a volunteer fireman, his spiky metal helmet haloed in orange flames.

Your folks own that building down there?

Yes.

Well – it's on fire.

Moments later, the three of you stood there – you, your mother, your father – in the driveway in your pajamas, watching flames leap up the utility lines, where they set off sparks. As the roof collapsed your atheist father put a hand to his sloped forehead.

My god, he said under his breath.

Later that same morning, you sifted through muck and ashes, pulling out boxes of waterlogged capacitors, a charred notebook, a drowned oscilloscope ... In a pile of soggy ashes and vermiculite something glittered like gold, a brass turning from one of the lathes. You put it in your pocket ...

AT DAWN, WITH your father snoring, you go down to the basement and empty the washing machine. The formerly white bed sheets are now beige. So are your mother's headpieces. You carry the latter up to the kitchen, where, seated in the breakfast nook, you try to clean them with a can of K2r Spot Lifter spray. When that doesn't do the trick you try a mixture of baking soda and vinegar. Using an old toothbrush you grind the paste in and around sequins, rhinestones, crinoline, and artificial pearls, the bristles working it into a froth. Finished, you carry the headpieces back downstairs and re-hang them back on the clothesline next to the furnace.

Back upstairs, hoping that it will help them dry faster, you set the house thermostat to broiling,

By then the sun is up. Birds sing.

You lie back down next to your still sleeping father.

Hours later, when you check the headpieces they're still wet.

They're also still beige. Worse, they smell like shit.

You spray them with Glade.

* * *

I DON'T SEE WHY IT SHOULD BE SO BLOODY DIFFICULT.

I know, Papa.

Fine – in that case do it, then. Increase the proportion.

I'm trying, Papa.

Don't try, do it, damn you!

It's not so simple, Papa.

What's not simple? All you have to do is increase the bloody proportion. That's all I'm asking of you, nothing more. Give me that satisfaction, why don't you? Is it asking so much? I don't see any good reason why you should deny me this one little thing!

No one's denying you anything.

Bloody …

It's just not so easy, that's all.

You're right, it's too complicated, your father says, shaking his head.

I'm sorry, Papa.

Too complicated.

I'm sorry.

Screw it!

Yes, that's right, Papa. Screw it!

Your father laughs and so do you.

ESPRESSO ON THE DOCK.

What do we remember? What do we know? Are knowledge and memory the same? Just because we remember something, does that mean that we know it? Is memory something that we possess, like knowledge, or is it something we do – an act?

According to one theory, the difference between knowledge and memory is like the difference between the molecules in the air and the wind that moves them. The molecules are facts, things known, ideas, images, and other types of information stored in the cells of our brains. When we remember something, in the act of remembering it and only through that action do we excite those bits of knowledge into what we call memories. Through the act of remembering, our memories aren't merely shaped, they're created.

As soon as we stop remembering, just as the wind stops existing when it stops blowing, our memories cease to exist.

Knowledge, on the other hand, is fixed in our minds until rendered obsolete by new knowledge, which usurps it.

> Given the interrupted character of memory, there seems to be no grounding in the narratives for the assumption that it is the same person who is remembered as who now remembers. And given the plural character of memory, it seems to be a fallacy to suppose that it is the same person who figures in all the different memory narratives one has.
>
> JOHN CAMPBELL
> *The Structure of Time in Autobiographical Memory*

The safest memories are the memories which are in the brains of people who cannot remember.

YADIN DUDAI, Weizmann Institute of Science, Israel

The visiting nurse reading to him from his beloved German dictionary. "Flugzeugwarnnetz." "Stadtverordnetenversammlungen." "Verbarrik adieren.""Leberknödelsuppe." "Fussballweltmeisterschaft."... Feeding him tapioca pudding and pea soup in the nursing home, where a picture of Pope John Paul II hangs over his bed.

* * *

"PAUL J. SELGIN, AGE 88, OF 75½ WOOSTER ST., BETHEL, *died Thursday, February 24, 2000, husband of Pinuccia (dePoli) Selgin.*

"Born in Milan, Italy, in 1912, he was the son of the late Guido and Julia (Treves) Senigaglia. He emigrated to the United States in the 1930s and graduated from Harvard University with a PhD in physics.

"Mr. Selgin taught engineering at Brooklyn Polytechnic Institute in the 1940s, and was later director of the Electronics Division of the U.S. Bureau of Standards in Washington, D.C.

"In 1957 he moved to Bethel, where he headed his own electronics laboratory, inventing, designing, and creating prototypes of quality control instruments, including the Thickness Gauge and the Color Coder, used by dozens of industries.

"Also a painter and author, Mr. Selgin wrote books that ranged in subject matter from electronic textbooks to science fiction novels to philosophical, linguistic, and etymological studies. In his later years he taught languages at Western Connecticut State University in Danbury.

"Besides his wife, he is survived by two sons, Peter Selgin of New York, NY, and George Selgin, PhD, of Athens, GA; two daughters, Ann Levy of St. Albans, VT, and Clare Wolfowitz of Chevy Chase, MD, and five grandchildren.

"A gathering of friends and relatives will be conducted at the Green Funeral Home, 57 Main St., Danbury, Monday afternoon from 2 to 3 p.m. Cremation will take place at the convenience of the family.

"Contributions may be made to the Bethel Ambulance Association, 38 South St., Bethel, CT 06801, or to the Danbury Animal Welfare Society, P.O. Box 971, Danbury CT 06813."

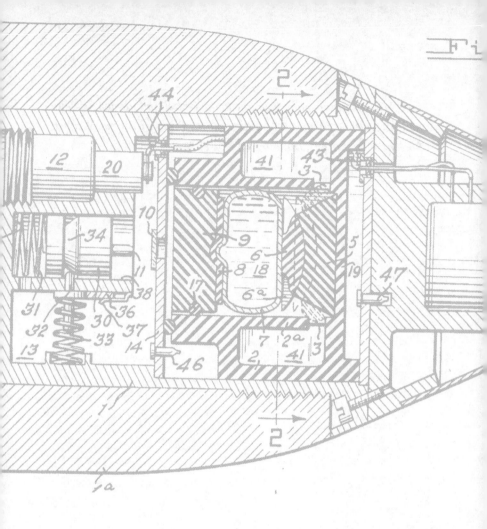

"RESERVE TYPE BATTERY," Patent No. 4,218,525

XXIV.
Green Funeral Home,
Danbury, Connecticut, 2000

GEORGE – BY THEN A FULL PROFESSOR AT THE UNIVER-
sity of Georgia – flew up for the service. Your brother had been
married for twenty years, divorced less than one. Though still a
dedicated bicyclist who did regular trips of fifty to a hundred miles,
thanks to his fondness for good wine and restaurant meals, he'd
put on some weight. He had a good twenty pounds over you. Still,
in his custom tailored (in Hong Kong, where he spent a year as a
visiting lecturer) suit and raw silk shirt he looked quite good. Your
brother's good looks often caught you by surprise. It was like looking in a mirror, one with a will and opinions of its own.

Together you and George planned your father's memorial
service, choosing relics to be displayed on the commemorative
altar – a folding banquet table draped with a red tablecloth, the
same items that you'd been gathering after the service when the
strange wintry woman confronted you with the information that
your father was Jewish.

The subject had been raised before. There had been that
remark by a cousin in Italy, and there'd been other suggestions,
rumors of distant Jewish origins in Austria – or was it some Slavic
nation? The one time you'd asked him directly, your father, great
scoffer that he was, scoffed at your inquiry, dismissing the sugges-
tion offhand. Aughh, don't be ridiculous, he'd said, or something
like that.

So neither side of your family was Jewish? you asked him.

He'd been sitting in his rocking chair when you asked. At first the question didn't seem to register. When it did, it didn't faze or catch him off guard in any way. It was as if you had presented him with an absurdity, a dish of ice cream sprinkled with electronic resistors. Your father pursed his lips, shook his head.

Aughh, he said. We were Catholic.

Yes, I know that, but might some of your ancestors have been –

Oh, no no no, he'd said, shaking his head vigorously (more vigorously, you would think in retrospect, than necessary), grimacing the way he did when entering lakes and other bodies of water to swim. Then the dismissive wave, as though your interrogations were a housefly pestering him. And that had been that until that woman at his funeral.

DO YOU SEE her? you asked George soon after the woman had gone.

Who?

That woman who was just here talking to me.

No. Why? Who was she?

An old German woman. She just walked up to me and said, "Did you know your father was Jewish?"

Your brother nodded dully.

Do you know anything about this?

I've had my suspicions, he said.

Like you your twin had questioned your ancestry. He'd even done some research. The findings added fuel to his suspicions. Before he'd re-invented it as "Selgin," your twin explained, your father's surname had been Senegaglia or Senigaglia. Senigallia is the name of a port city on Italy's Adriatic coast, George went on to say. With very few exceptions, Italians who share their last names with those of port cities are – if not Jewish – of Jewish origin, George said.

How long have you know this?

At least twenty years, said George with a shrug.

Where did you learn it?

One of our cousins probably told me (the same maternal

cousin, you assumed, who had noted the downward curve of your nostrils). Then I checked up on it. It's true. Senegalia was a common Jewish surname. It's been around at least eight hundred years, since the Renaissance. Papa's parents were either Jews or descended from them.

Did you ever try to talk to Papa about this?

I tried. Once.

And what did he say?

He insisted that there was no connection whatsoever, that his family's surname had nothing to do with the port city, that it was just a coincidence.

A coincidence? And you believed him?

Why shouldn't I have? He'd never lied to me before, not that I knew of.

How come you never talked to me about this?

Why should I have? Anyway, I didn't think it was that important.

You didn't think it was *important?*

No, I didn't.

Why would our father have told some German woman that he's Jewish but not his own children?

I have no idea, George said as he packed away your father's typewriter. And honestly I don't give a damn.

You don't think it's strange?

Who knows? Maybe she forced it out of him. Gestapo tactics. *Ve hev ah veys.*

That's not even slightly funny.

It all makes perfect sense if you ask me, George said with another shrug. Our pacifist Anglophile Papa cozying up to his Teutonic *Fräulein.* Maybe he wanted to appease her. Like Neville Chamberlain and Hitler.

IN THE TERRACED backyard of your mother's house, you spoke with Clare, one of your two half-sisters, who had come up from Washington, D.C., for the service. In your whole life you'd seen her and Ann maybe a dozen times, almost as infrequently as their father.

Ann and Clare had both married Jewish men. Ann's husband, Jim, with whom she lived in St. Albans, Vermont, was a Columbia graduate and lawyer. Clare married Paul Wolfowitz.[8] Unlike her sister, Clare was a practicing Jew, having converted to Judaism after her marriage.

You told Clare about the strange woman and her claim, which you called "crazy."

There's nothing crazy about it, Clare said. Papa was Jewish.

You've known all along?

Since I was a teenager. Why? Are you just realizing that now?

Did he tell you?

God, no. Papa never talked about it. We just sort of figured it out.

You and Ann?

Clare nodded.

How?

Clare shook her head. She had a gaunt pretty face with your father's large deep-set eyes and aquiline nose. There were lots of clues, she said. It didn't take a rocket scientist to put them together.

Why would he deny it in the first place?

I'm sure he had his reasons. Being a Jew wasn't exactly easy back in those days – not that it ever was. His mother converted to Catholicism. She hired a series of English nannies for him. I guess he took her desire to assimilate to the next level. Papa always thought of himself as English, since he was little. I think he fell in love with one of his nannies. When he came here and changed his name, that was it, the last step on the way to reinventing himself. By then there was really nothing left of his Jewish past for him to deny, not consciously, anyway.

He lied to us, you said. To me and George.

What did you ask him?

---

8   The former ambassador to Indonesia and Dean at Johns Hopkins, future Undersecretary of Defense for the second Bush administration.

We asked him if our ancestors were Jewish.

You might as well have asked him if they were primates. Anyway, I don't think he lied. I'm sure he didn't think he was lying. When he said his family wasn't Jewish, I'm sure he believed it. I'm sure he never thought of himself as a Jew. It just wasn't part of his self-definition.

Clare's theory made some sense. Still, it seemed paradoxical if not perverse that both daughters of a man intent on eradicating his Jewish origins married Jews. The far-flung apples had found their way back to the tree.

I still don't get it, you said. If it were anyone else I'd understand, but Papa? He was always so rational. He worshipped at the altar of logic and reason. They were as close to an almighty god as he ever got. He was honest to a fault.

No kidding, said Clare. He could be brutally honest.

How could someone as honest and rational turn a blind eye on facts?

To you it may seem irrational, Clare replied. But you need to look at it from Papa's perspective. From his perspective the idea of being a Jew made no sense. To our father *that* would have been irrational. It just didn't compute. As far as Papa was concerned he was an English atheist.

YOU SPOKE WITH Ann, your other half-sister. Her version of things differed.

We knew nothing – ever, Ann said. If Clare knew anything, she must have learned it very recently. I sure didn't know, though I'm not exactly shocked either. I mean I knew the whole thing about Italians with place names of cities and all that. Jim's mom pointed that out to me.

Your mother-in-law?

She was on a mission. For years she did her best to convince me that our father was Jewish. She kept a dossier, a whole file folder filled with newspaper articles about Jewish Italians clipped from the *New York Times.* She'd photocopy and send them to me. But I paid no attention to them or her.

Why not?

She was a Jewish mother-in-law. Naturally, she wanted my father to be Jewish!

That's about all I knew, Ann said, that and that Papa left the Catholic Church when he was eighteen. The nuns kept refusing to answer his questions about science.

For sure our mother couldn't have known, Ann went on. If she'd known she would have told us. We were the only non-Jews in our neighborhood. Eighty-sixth and Riverside. One day, I remember, we were celebrating United Nations Day. Everyone in our school class had to stand up and say where their parents were from. All the parents of our classmates were Holocaust survivors. Clare and I stood out. We didn't belong. We'd have given anything to say we were Jewish.

* * *

WITH GEORGE BACK IN GEORGIA, IT WAS LEFT TO YOU to scatter your father's ashes. You considered scattering them along one of the many abandoned railway beds your father took you and George hiking along when you were seven or eight, possibly in the craggy tunnel where a hornet once bit you on the cheek, assuming you could find it.

Instead you scattered the ashes under a laurel bush at Huntington State Park, a few dozen yards from the big rock from which you and the teacher plunged naked to swim to the island with the miniature stone decorative lighthouse. As you scattered the ashes, a sudden gust blew them over the tips of the nearly new white sneakers you were wearing, the ones your father bought for himself the day he suffered his first stroke.

You were carrying the empty plastic urn back to the car when it struck you that all that remained of your father now were memories that time, too, would scatter like dust. Then there'd be nothing left.

As you drove back to your mother's house, you vowed to learn all you could about your father.

* * *

WORKING AT A SERIES OF DESKS STREWN WITH PHOTO-graphs, newspaper clippings, letters, patent applications, immigration records, and other documents, bit by bit, like an air crash investigator reconstructing the fuselage of a downed passenger jet, you pieced together the shards of your father's past.

BEGIN EACH CHAPTER WITH A VIGNETTE, MEMORY, IN-sight, idea ... *something close to narrator's present life – like letter writing. Episodes of present inform/reflect the past.*

Style: The simpler the plumage, the more elaborate the bower; the simpler the bower, the fancier the plumage.

Nothing in particular (nothing really) happening at all with these words. Poems don't do anything. Not supposed to. "I, too, dislike it."

I'd like to abandon everything I've believed about writing and start over. A new tack. Like a sailboat coming around. Here we go! Watch out for the boom! First, I'd do away with all forms of dramatization, the first step toward sentimentality, that greatest of evils. And then the whole idea of heroes and even of protagonists and characters. In this new style of writing there'd be only the narrator, no one else. Huysmans got it right. The narrator as anonymous voice making declarations. The world is as pronounced, nothing more or less. I narrate, there-fore I am. *Scene-painting is garbage. Things just are. Not as the nouveau romanists had it or tried to have it, objectively, but as a series of stated perceptions rather than as objects. Too late for objectivity. Narrator as the voice of subjective truth, declaring things not as they are but as they appear to be.*

I don't build a house without predicting an end to the present social order.

F. LLOYD WRIGHT

Every angel is terrible.

RILKE

The diminishment of the sense of wonderment that comes with age is no less perilous than the loss of memory, agility, sight, hearing, or any of the other senses, but more tragic. A chunk of potato at the end of a fork is an insignificant object to an adult; to a four-year-old it rates among the Seven Wonders of the Natural World. If four-year-olds could write what they think and feel they'd all be poets.

Shadows playing like vermin on the sidewalk.

A sunset equivalent in its palette to embarrassment.

How psychic storms churn the bottom silt of the mind with its vast riches and sunken treasures. The power of touching bottom.

Let me go with my dark darling into myself.

DICKEY

Mother's ashtray ("Leave alone de ashtray!"), the centerpiece of the coffee table, the sun of our childhood solar system. A four-sided porcelain cube, each side displaying the package design for a 1920s Italian cigarette brand: Macedonia / Due Palme / Seraglio / Edelweiss. *In addition to her lipstick-stained cigarette butts, mom's ashtray held within its corners the essence of the Mediterranean, a whisper of the Levant, the dry winds of the sirocco: the four angels holding back the four winds of the earth. Long after she quit smoking it remained there, on that coffee table, a symbol of her exotic origins, until she hurled it at the mirrored cabinet across the room during one of her fights with Papa, smashing it to bits.*

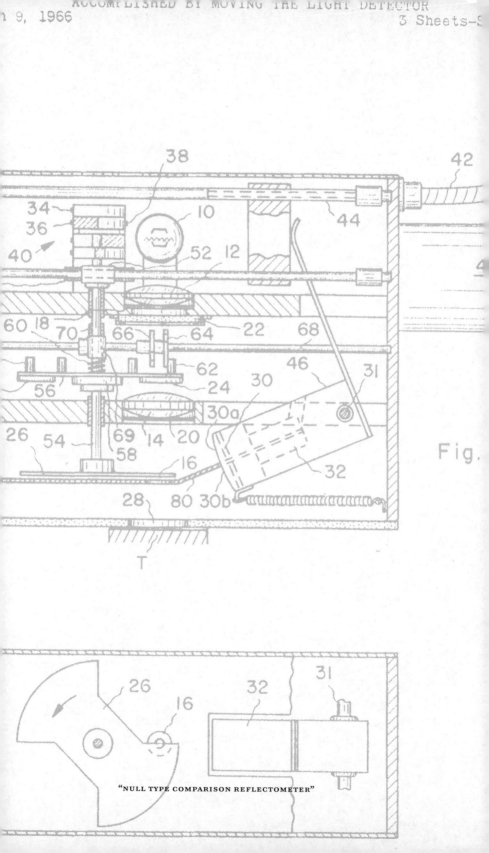

Fig.

"NULL TYPE COMPARISON REFLECTOMETER"

XXV.
The *Supreme*
England, Summer 1934

How to be happy, to invent ourselves,
shedding the inertia of the past?
SVETLANA BOYM, *The Future of Nostalgia*

ACCORDING TO BIRTH ACT NO. 332, AS WITNESSED AND recorded by Giuseppe Silva, official of the *Stato Civile* acting as delegated Secretary of the Mayor, in the year One Thousand Nine-Hundred Twelve on the second day of February at 3:10 p.m. in the Town Hall of the City of Milan,

> there came before me one Guido Sinigaglia [sp.], of Austrian citizenship, age forty, employee, residing in Milano, to inform me that at 11:45 a.m. on the 28ᵗʰ of the prior month in the house located at Via Legnano 28 to one Giulia Treves of the upper class (his wife, living with him) was born a baby boy whom he did not present to me, and to whom is given the name: Paolo Guiseppe.[9]

According to a handwritten note appended years later to the lower margin of the birth record, *Sinigaglia Paolo Giuseppe* was "considered to be of the Hebrew race, because he was born of parents considered to be of the Hebrew race, as resulted in the racial census of 22 August 1938."

* * *

---

9   "To the act noted above were present also as witnesses Enrico Bordiga, aged 49, a building superintendent, and Antonio Tognotta Galli, aged 42, also a building superintendent, both residents of the town.
"Having received evidence of the birth of the child for health reasons the informant was excused from bringing the child before the Mayor's secretary."

YOUR FATHER DESCENDED FROM TWO PROMINENT FAM-
ilies, both Jewish: the Senigaglia or Sinigaglia family on his father's
side, the Treves family on his mother's.[10]

The Senigaglia name is most probably of Roman origin, dat-
ing back to 1215, when the Fourth Council of the Lateran decreed
(Canon #67, "Jews and excessive Usury"):

> *The more the Christian religion is restrained from usurious practices,*
> *so much the more does the perfidy of the Jews grow in these matters, so*
> *that within a short time they are exhausting the resources of Christians.*
> *Wishing therefore to see that Christians are not savagely oppressed by*
> *Jews in this matter, we ordain by this synodal decree that if Jews in*
> *future, on any pretext, extort oppressive and excessive interest from*
> *Christians, then they are to be removed from contact with Christians*
> *until they have made adequate satisfaction for the immoderate burden.*

Over the next few centuries, many Roman Jews left Rome
for smaller villages and towns where they established small usury
banks. One of these towns was Senigallia (or "Sinigallia," in Old
Italian) in the Provence of Ancona on Italy's Adriatic coast. Much
of that town's appeal to Jews lay in its proximity to water, which
provided an open escape route and made them feel safer.

After 1503, however, following further decrees against Jews
(including one requiring them to wear yellow badges), many fled
Senigallia in favor of smaller, more hidden interior towns. One of
these was Gorizia, a *commune* north of Trieste that to this day is
heavily populated by Jews. Many of your relatives are to be found
in a cemetery there.

It was in Gorizia that our grandfather, Guido Senigaglia, was
born along with ten brothers and sisters. Among these were Arri-
go Avraham Senigaglia, who, together with his sister Lucia Lea,
perished in Auschwitz in 1943. Another was Gilberto Senigaglia,
a Trieste physician/gynecologist who presided over the births of

---

10   Spellings of my father's original surname conflict. The birth record spells it Sinigaglia,
      with an i; according to nearly all other documents and records, it's Senigaglia, with
      an e.

James and Nora Joyce's children. He may also have tutored Joyce in Italian.[11]

As for his brother Guido, your father's father, he worked for the now defunct Credito Italiano in Milan. He was a punctilious record keeper, keeping track of every penny earned and spent, spending hour after hour in his study balancing his books. In the evenings he'd play Scopa and Briscola with his mother-in-law, and though the stakes were extremely low and no money passed between them, Guido Senigaglia took careful note of their wins and losses in a blue ledger book kept strictly for that purpose. Having never achieved his lifelong dream of being promoted to director of the bank, he died in his sixty-sixth year, in 1934. No record exists documenting the cause of this meticulous record-keeper's death. Still, no evidence suggests that he was run over by a tram.

And though your father claimed he was an only child, he did in fact have a sister. Her name was Berta Conti. She was born in 1902, ten years before your father's birth – out of wedlock, presumably, which would explain his knowing nothing about her.[12]

Theories conflict as to the origin of your grandmother's surname. One theory traces it to the medieval town of Troyes, France, where Shlomo Yitzchaki (or Rashi, as he was better known), a rabbi famed for his lucid commentaries on the Talmud, lived. A second theory derives the name from Treviso, near Venice. A third connects it with the town of Trier, Germany ("Trèves" in French).

Wherever its origins, throughout the fourteenth and sixteenth centuries the Treves line spread through Europe. Among the Treves who settled in Italy were Johanan B. Joseph Treves, whose son Raphael Joseph became a publisher of books. By the end of the nineteenth century, the Treves Brothers of Milan ("Fratelli Trev-

---

11   "The reason I write in Italian to Giorgio," Joyce wrote years later in a letter to his daughter, "is not to conceal anything from your keen swift flashing and infallible eye but because when he was introduced to me 30 years ago by Dr. Gilberto Sinigaglia [sic] I said: Toh! Georgio. To which he replied: Baaaa boooo. Our conversation has continued in that tongue."

     Babu = a Hindy gentleman + babbo (daddy), illuminating the phrase "the boys of wetford hail him babu" in Chapter 1.6 of *Finnegans Wake*.

12   I found no information concerning her death.

es") was the largest publishing firm in Italy, publishers of Piran-
dello and Gabriele D'Annunzio – the poet, bon vivant, seducer,
war-monger, and inspirer of Mussolini and other fascists. Nonnie,
your grandmother, Giulietta Treves, was the daughter of Michele
Treves, brother to the famous publishers.

Your father's maternal great-aunt, Anette Treves, married
Enrico Levi. Their son was the writer and painter Carlo Levi, who
wrote *Christ Stopped at Eboli*.

Not once while he lived did your father ever breathe a word
to you about these or any other members of his – your – family. They
were kept hidden from you, their existences not just uncelebrated,
but unknown. It was something like those dreams to which occupants of undersized dwellings are susceptible, where an unnoticed
door gives way to a series of sumptuous rooms – rooms that had
been there all along, only you never knew it. To those sumptuous
rooms your father held – or withheld – the keys.

Why had he sealed off all those rooms? Shame? Anger?
Neglect? Your half-sister Clare's theories failed to satisfy you. And
so, armed with a faded black-and-white photograph of a sailboat,
you arrived at some theories of your own.

* * *

THE TORN, FADED BLACK-AND-WHITE PHOTO SHOWS AN
elegant sailboat plying the waters of an estuary under cloudy skies
with a bank of marsh weeds in the background. Manning the helm
in what looks like a suit is your future-father. Another man stands
next to him. At the bottom of the photo the inscription in faded
fountain pen ink reads:

> *Just to remind you*
> *Summer 1934*
> *John H. Goddard*
> *"SUPREME"*

You first saw the photo in the Building during one of your
childhood visits there, tucked between the pages of a German
novel in the bookcase in the back room where your father kept the

trundle bed in case of a bad fight with your mother. Years later, per your request, he mailed you the photograph along with an accompanying letter.

The sailboat, he explained in the letter, was a sloop he and six others chartered during the summer of 1934 – the year his father died. Her name was the *Supreme*. They sailed her through the Norfolk Broads, a system of rivers, lakes, and canals that form a network through Norfolk, a low-lying county northeast of London.

Your father had been to England before, several times starting in 1927, when at fifteen he spent part of a summer alone there, in London. Of that first summer alone your father recalled only random details. On the Channel crossing after dinner he got seasick and threw up over the rail. As he wiped his mouth, a Scot who had been standing nearby said to him, "You should ne'er part wi' wha' you've paid for."

On that first visit he had been struck by London's immensity, by its seas of small houses, not *palazzo* apartments like those familiar to him in Milan, but semi-detached brick homes in neat curved rows, with small gardens in the front and potted chimneys stretching up and downhill far as his eyes could see, crisscrossed by scores of railway tracks, all converging – or seeming to – at a place called Clapham Junction, "the very symbol of banality – but not to a 15-year-old boy from Italy." So your father wrote to you in his letter featuring a rare glimpse into his past. From Clapham Junction:

> a municipal rail, a bridge, Victoria. Then a taxi ride, the red buses and the calm of it all: no yelling, no hooting like Paris taxicabs, not even that much traffic.

Your future-father stayed at a manor house called Hepworth Hall. Weather permitting, meals were served in the garden where the chutney bowl squirmed with wasps. He spent his days riding a rented bicycle, taking outings to Cambridge and Clacton-on-Sea, where, "for two-and-six," through a telescope on an amusement pier, instead of peering out across Martello Bay, he spied on the girls walking along the boardwalk. Finding one he liked, he caught up with her and confessed having watched her through the telescope. This novel line apparently worked: they spent the rest of that afternoon together, swimming and sunbathing, strolling the shore and eating ice cream cones.

After a week your future-tense-father traded Hepworth Hall for a boarding house in Kilburn, then still a working-class London neighborhood. The landlady had a pretty but disturbed daughter. She spent all of her days alone in her room wearing a frazzled scarlet nightgown, singing the same mournful ditty over and over:

> *I'm unhappy, so unhappy, everything is wrong*
> *Bluebird, sing me a song ...*

At the boarding house he met a French traveler his age named Maurice who'd mastered the trick of putting French five-cent coins (the size of British pennies but worth a lot less) into subway turnstiles. Together they roamed London. You could imagine how excited your future-father must have been, as excited as you were the first time on your own in New York City. Romance, sex, the intrigues offered by not just a city, but a foreign city. By the time you knew him, your father had a paunch; his hair was already thin and gray. But the father who roamed the foggy streets of London in your mind with his French sidekick was slim and fit. His hair was dark, rich, and curly like yours, brushed back from a sloped forehead, his large, gray, deep-set eyes darting from one unfamiliar object to the next, aglow with curiosity, with the possibilities held by new things.

The man at the helm of the *Supreme* is just a few years older and even more handsome. The sailing trip, which your father's mother funded, had been his graduation gift. He'd just earned his undergraduate degree in engineering from the Polytechnic University of Milan (*Politecnico di Milano*), the oldest in Milan and the most highly respected technical university in the world.

"The man with me in the photograph," your father's letter to you continues,

> is David Fitt, my good friend for many years, a lawyer and a real
> gentleman. The photo was taken by John Goddard, who signed and

dated it. ... We were a group of 7, I think, when we started out [on the voyage], but only 3 stuck it out to the end. When we were 7 my job was folding blankets, but with only 3 of us each did a little bit of everything. I cooked risotto once but it was no great success. In spite of the risotto and the blankets I really had a great time ... We sailed all the way to Great Yarmouth at the mouth of the Yare on the North Sea, a place well-known for "bloaters," a fish people eat for breakfast.

The letter goes on to describe how the washing water they pumped from the estuary into a tank had been phosphorescent. "It was weird to wash your hands and face in it." Sailing had been difficult. The canals were narrow, making tacking and sailing against the wind impossible. In the shallows the *Supreme* ran aground frequently. "There was a pole you used to push the boat off the shoals," your father wrote,

I did this once, but when I got the boat moving whoever was at the tiller managed to catch the wind and left me stranded, hanging on the pole which was stuck in the mud. This was enormously funny and after feeling let down for a moment I joined in the general laughter.

At a place called Beccles, while swimming in a river, your father met a girl he liked. But the *Supreme* had a schedule to follow, and the rest of the crew grew impatient with his flirting. With great sadness he'd been forced to leave her.

Contrary to your image of your father, the photo of the *Supreme* and the story that went with it demonstrated to you that he hadn't always been such a loner, someone incapable of intimate friendships. The father you grew up knowing had few real friends. Apart from his secret mistresses, his most intimate relations were with fellow members of the AMC – the Appalachian Mountain Club – with whom he'd go hiking on weekends, or fellow Unitarians at the so-called Barn, where, at the secular Sunday services, he might hope to encounter an atheist or two. Then there was the Arion Society, a club devoted to German culture. He would volunteer at their *Faschingballs* – costumed carnival dances – serving bratwurst and tearing tickets from a roll, enjoying the costumes, beer, *oom-pah* music, and German conversation. But sooner or later all these organizations and their activities bored him, and your father would retreat to his beloved Building, to his snakes and spiders and inventions-in-progress.

How different the man at the tiller of that sailboat: handsome, carefree, flirtatious – a twenty-two-year-old like many twenty-two-year-olds. Like you, but more certain of his direction, less confused.

And though he had seen fit to give you this rare intimate glimpse into that English summer, the rest of your father's life before you were born – his Italian childhood, his years in the U.S. before meeting your mother, his first two marriages, remained, for all intents and purposes, a dark secret, one that – for all its brightness – the photograph of the *Supreme* rendered darker still. Like the concentrated beam of a flashlight, in illuminating one portion of your father's past it shed ever more obscurity over the others.

This obscurity took the form of questions. Chief among these: why did your father, an Italian Jew, choose to reinvent himself as an English atheist?

THEORY #1: ANGLOPHILIA

The sail outing aboard the *Supreme* took place in the summer of 1934. The Third Reich had yet to adopt the Nuremburg Laws; they would not be passed until September 1935. Five more years would pass before Mussolini signed his so-called "Pact of Steel" with Hitler. Still, by the summer of 1934 the precarious position of all Jews throughout Eastern and Central Europe was – or should have been – obvious.

Seeking relative safety, waves of Jews flooded Great Britain, arriving there only to confront a different set of Blackshirts, those of the British Union of Fascists, the B.U.F. When not attacking Jews with fists and boots, the B.U.F. denounced them through loudspeakers and murderous slogans scrawled on walls.

This was the England where Paolo Senigaglia felt at home.

Still, there were practical reasons for choosing England. Thanks to a succession of British nannies hired for him by his mother, from a very young age the man who was to become your father spoke English fluently. And England was easy to get to: a series of trains from Milan to Paris, then one from Paris to the channel boat.

But something beyond safety and proximity attracted your father to England. From when he was a young boy he had been drawn to English ways and people in part thanks to the books he read – Kipling, *The Forsyte Saga*, and *The Road to Wigan Pier* – novels in English that he got from the library. One quality of those books may have appealed to him above all others, an essence that seeped out of the prose in which they were written, the quality conveyed by Charles Chaplin's cane-spinning walk and credulous facial expressions: that blend of reasonable restraint and total lack of presumption best captured by the word *decent* as in "a decent chap."

It was this quality of reasonable restraint above all others that drew your father to the English and England, a quality whose antithesis was exemplified by the bombastic rhetoric of fascism under Mussolini – the prime minister who once kissed your volleyball champion future-mother on the cheek.

Paolo Giusseppe Senigaglia's embrace of English values was, or may well have been, to a large extent, his means of revolt against the two sources of tyranny that bore down on him throughout his childhood and youth: Italian fascism and an overprotective mother. Throw in a long-legged English nanny on whom he'd had an unrequited pubescent crush and you have a surefire recipe for Anglophilia.

THEORY #2: ANTI-SEMITISM

You'd heard him rail against televangelists, coffee creamers that didn't pour properly, and peanut butter (*vile, loathsome substance!*), but apart from that one occasion when prompted by a black man's presence in a sought-after telephone booth he uttered a racial slur, you never suspected your father of prejudice. Prejudices were irrational, after all, and your father was a rational man – an engineer, a man of logical, scientific bent.

Yet when given expression, your father's disavowal of religious values of any sort was hardly measured or scientific. Why did such fury attach itself to it? Why this need to not merely disavow but deplore religions, as if they posed a threat to his survival?

Perhaps they did. Having jettisoned – first through his renouncement of the Catholic Church and then through his denial of any Jewish origins – any and all religious traditions, values, and beliefs, having thus forfeited membership in any religious tribe, he came to resent all religions. Instead of mourning his loss, he scorned those who hadn't endured it, who still belonged to something bigger than themselves.

Hence your future-father became a "self-loathing Jew," i.e., an anti-Semite. Was not his embrace of England and English values itself anti-Semitic? And what of his love of Germans, of their ludicrously long words, their books and beer and bratwurst and *oom-pah* music, not to mention at least one woman named Bernice?

Yet you never heard an anti-Semitic remark issue from your father's lips. You never once heard him say an unkind thing about a Jew or Jews. Still, you could not entirely discredit this theory.

Did David Fitt and his other crewmates on the *Supreme* have any idea that your future-father was Jewish? Had they even known that he was Italian? If his accent then was what you grew up knowing, though they may have guessed that he wasn't English, they would have been hard-pressed to infer his origins.

Maybe the risotto gave him away.

THEORY #3: THE DESIRE TO REINVENT HIMSELF

On the other hand, maybe your future-father's break with his birth country and family had nothing to do with anti-Semitism or Anglophilia. Maybe it was the result of the simple wish to reinvent himself, to start fresh, to open himself to new possibilities?

Mysterious illegitimate sister notwithstanding, your father was, after all, an only child, an overprotected one, with an only child's curiosity, imagination, and inventiveness. Combined with his extraordinary intelligence, that inventiveness would have led naturally to a desire to try new things, to explore fresh horizons, to refute, resist, or renounce things that might hold him back. Belonging to a tribe of any sort was certainly one of those things. Religion was another. So was patriotism in all its forms.

But of all the things that stood to hold your future-father back, none was more powerful than his mother. Italian mothers are known to be overprotective, especially of their male children. The Italian's have a special word for it: *mammone*, a mother's boy, those who keep their dear mothers forever and always in close proximity, there to advise them in all matters while darning their socks and doing their laundry.

And while it's true that your father never entirely escaped the fate of a *mammone*, he did at least manage to escape Italy, a land where children lived with or close to their parents until they died, where sons took up the occupations of their fathers and of their father's fathers, where to reinvent oneself was next to impossible.

Is it any wonder that your father fell in love with England? Is it any more of a wonder that he wound up in the United States of America, where he hoped to encounter all the good qualities of England minus the rabid anti-Semitism and the stifling class system, the one place left in the world where a man could truly hope to reinvent himself?

Hence on June 12, 1935, less than a year after his "Supreme" summer, on the passenger liner *Rex*, Paolo Giuseppe Senigaglia embarked from the port of Genoa for the United States of America.

I'M NOT INCLINED TO SPEAK OF THE AFFAIR THAT SEP-*arated me from my daughter. Who would be? The woman was some-one I met at a conference in Boston – or maybe Seattle – while living in upstate New York – or maybe it was Florida. Anyhow, I was living over a thousand miles away from my child and her mother, who was earning a graduate degree in Illinois, a pursuit that was to have kept us apart for three years, starting the year Audrey was born. Thanks to my stupidity – my lust, my loneliness, my greed, my indiscretion, my inability to understand what I really wanted … whatever you'd like to call it … three years turned into forever.*

I said I don't like to speak about it. That was honest enough. Then again, what's there to say? The rest is banalities and clichés. The real question is: how am I to forgive the person who condemned me to this lovely exile, myself? A confession seems a good way to start. Not to the affair. That's nothing; that takes a sentence, maybe two. To this whole existence of mine so far. That takes a book.

Whether we want it or not, for better or worse, our deeper nature usually gets what it wants, or thinks it wants. Blindness with respect to the forces, events, and influences that have shaped that nature leads to many if not most of our worst decisions. Since the two men for whom I felt the deepest affection were exiled by choice and/or circumstance, I have put myself in exile. By no coincidence am I, essentially, alone.

The worst form of exile is from the self. From that one problem all kinds of ills arise, including the inability to forgive that which we can't begin to understand.

It has taken me forever to write this book, which is to say that it has taken me forever to know myself, which is to say it has taken me forever to forgive myself. I should apologize, I guess, but to whom?

On bad days I say to myself, "Fuck me in a whole bunch of colors if this is my life." On good days I can't believe my luck.

A thing that concerns me: that what I've written is on one hand too polished, on the other too personal. Polished on the surface, hollow inside. How would you like that for an epitaph?

An old trick, build the critique into the opus, a preemptive strike.

READERS WILL DEMAND some form of closure, they'll have every right to ask, "What ultimate effect did learning about your father's past have on you? Has it changed you in some significant way? How?"

Honest answer: I'm not sure. I think in order to love others you must trust them, and in order to trust them you need to trust yourself, and in order to trust yourself you have to know yourself, and to know yourself you need not only to know and accept but to embrace the forces, events, traditions, and other circumstances that made you who you are.

IN HIS 1897 monograph on suicide, sociologist Emile Durkheim singled out abandonment of tribalism as the root cause of most of society's ills. He coined the term anomie, *meaning "a condition in which society provides little moral guidance to individuals," a breakdown of the social bonds in a community arising from a disjunction between purely personal and wider social values.*

Through scientific study, Durkheim demonstrated that in turn-of-the-century France the majority of suicides were Protestants, agnostics, and atheists – those without tribal affiliations. Since they didn't suffer from anomie, *Catholics and Jews were far less likely to kill themselves.*

It is through our relationship to the larger social order – our tribe – that we know and accept ourselves, that we feel the ground solid beneath our feet and know tomorrow will be another day much like today. The Jewish people never abandoned their tribe. Torah readings, Shabbat, staying kosher, candles before sundown, dipping in the mik-

vah – these are but a few of the "irrational" acts by which people of Jewish faith cling to their tribalism.

It was that tribalism that my father's parents relinquished in converting to Catholicism, and that my father obliterated every remaining trace of, preferring instead to be his own point of reference, the center of his world, a slave of anomie. In reinventing himself he broke a chain of ritual stretching across four thousand years. Once that chain has been broken it's impossible to mend. You have to build a new chain.

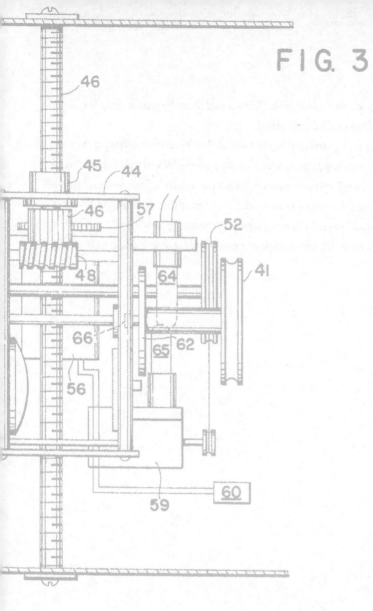

FIG. 3

46

45 44

46 57

52

64 41

48

66

65 62

56

59 60

"OPTICAL GAUGE FOR MEASURING THE THICKNESS OF A CONTINUOUS WEB."
From Patent No. 3,518,441

XXVI.

The Invention of Memory
United States, 1935 – 1957

ACCORDING TO THE *REX'S* PASSENGER MANIFEST, YOUR future-father's age was twenty-three; his occupation: engineer; his last permanent residence: Milan; his nearest relative: Giulia Treves (his mother); his destination: New York City; his expected duration of stay: permanent; his height: 5' 5"; complexion: natural; hair: brown; distinguishing marks: none. The manifest further attests that your future father was born on January 29, 1912; that he was able to read and write; that his passage was being paid for by himself; that he was in possession of over $50; that he had never been in the United States before; that he would not be joining any relative or friend; that he'd never been in prison or an almshouse; that he was not a Polygamist or an Anarchist; that he was not crippled or deformed; and that had not come to labor in the United States by reason of any offer, solicitation, promise, or agreement, express or implied. [13]

From the *Rex's* deck rail, like so many before him, your future-father was awestruck by the Manhattan cityscape, a forest of art-deco skyscrapers stretching infinitely upward toward some unspecified glorious ideal. How beautiful the city of New York looked to him then, and how disappointed he would be to discover, after passing through Ellis Island, that contrary to his fantasies the streets of America, or anyhow of New York City, were paved "not with gold, but with uneven, potholed layers of garbage-

---

13   Our father was 5'7".

strewn cobblestones and asphalt, with dirty newspapers and coffee cups blowing everywhere."

His first U.S. address was a few blocks east of Columbia University, in a residence called Warren Hall, whose occupants spent
their free time sitting in chairs on the roof, filling the air with intellectual talk and aromatic smoke from their pipes. This is the scene
that with minor variations would recreate itself for you in a dream
that you had about your father not long after his death (though in
the dream he's smoking a cigarette, not a pipe, and he's alone. But
he's on a rooftop in a city, and young).

From New York your future-father moved to Cambridge,
Massachusetts, where he bought his first American car, a '29 Ford
convertible with a droll rumble seat. From 1935 to 1936 he attended the Division of Engineering and Applied Sciences at Harvard
Graduate School. When not engaged in his research he'd borrow a
wherry (wider than a racing skull, with a sliding seat for fast row-
ing) from the boating club. When the Charles River froze over in
winter, he skated on it.

In the summer of 1936, offered a well-paying job with RCA,
Paolo Senigaglia quit Harvard and moved from Cambridge to East
Orange, New Jersey, near Edison's laboratory. He rented a corner
room in a gabled Victorian house on Prospect Street. He loved the
New Jersey suburbs, with their big trees and green, sloping lawns.[14]

The RCA job was his first salaried position. So alien was the
concept of a paycheck to your future-father, it would have slipped
his mind completely had a fellow employee not instructed him to
report to the payroll window.

He worked – not very hard – in a quality-control laboratory.
His supervisor was a woman with a good sense of humor and the
atmosphere was relaxed. Most of the other employees were women,
too. When at the end of the workday he watched them stream out of
the factory gate, it was, as he put it in a letter to Margaret, his sec-

---

14   For the rest of his life, people called my father "Doctor Selgin." And though he scoffed
at the honorific, he never contradicted them or denied having a Harvard PhD. He never completed his dissertation and graduated with a Master's of Science degree in applied engineering.

ond wife, "quite a show, like a musical, almost, a Hollywood spectacular, unlike anything at an Italian factory gate." On weekends, in Manasquan near Asbury Park, with some of his coworkers, he swam in the surf, picnicked, and sang Gilbert and Sullivan songs.

He returned to Italy just long enough to bring his mother back to the States, departing again on the *Rex* from Naples in February of 1939. Though as it did back in '35, the *Rex's* manifest lists his name as Paolo "Senigaglia" (with the silent second g accidentally omitted but corrected by hand), by then your future father was already using his Anglicized name: Paul Selgin, the new surname his invention of which he was inordinately proud. Not only was "Selgin" unique, unlike the original with its clandestine mute consonant it was – or should have been – easier to pronounce.[15]

Your future-father's second time in the United States differed markedly from the first. America was bracing itself for war. An atmosphere of restlessness, restraint, and regulation prevailed. The freedoms he had enjoyed during his first visit were not to be reclaimed. Jobs were scarcer, too. Unable to find work at an electronics firm, he took a job as an instructor at what was then the Polytechnic Institute of Brooklyn – or Brooklyn Poly, as it was known. While teaching there and living in a dingy basement apartment in Brooklyn Heights, Paul Selgin wrote the series of lectures that would become his first and only published book.[16]

In New York City he encountered all kinds of people, not just other engineers, but architects, painters, photographers, and filmmakers. It tickled you to imagine your father in those days, hob-

---

15   Or so its inventor assumed, until people kept pronouncing the g hard rather than soft. To remedy this, he took to saying, "Like Elgin, as in Elgin Marbles, but with an s," thinking – wrongly – that the g in Elgin was soft when it was hard. Then again, no one seemed to know how to pronounce Elgin, as in Elgin Marbles, either. Throughout their lives, along with him, his children would endure hearing their name constantly mispronounced.

16   Electrical Transmission in Steady State. The lectures were sponsored by the so-called "War Training Program." Officially known as the "Engineering, Science, and Management War Training" program, or the ESMWT, it was one of the largest, most successful government-sponsored educational programs in U.S. history, second only to the G.I. Bill. From 1942 – 1945 it provided, free of charge, college-level courses to thousands of Americans to help fill civilian technical and scientific positions vacated by the draft.

nobbing with Greenwich Village bohemians as you would consort with them decades later. You pictured him in an open-necked plaid shirt and beret, a cross between Maynard Krebs and Jon Gnagy.

All this was before America entered the war. Not long after it did, on a skiing trip to Interlaken in neutral Switzerland, while riding on a ski lift alongside her (so you imagined), your future-father met the Englishwoman named Betty who would become his first wife and with whom he would father your half-sisters, Ann and Clare. Their marriage lasted seven years, its end occasioned by your future-father's sexual dalliances, his wish to relocate from Fort Wayne, Indiana, to Washington, D.C., and most of all by his insistence that his mother come live with them there.

Unable to find another well-paying job anywhere on the East Coast, your future-father took another instructorship, this one at Purdue University in Fort Wayne, Indiana. With his mother left behind in the Brooklyn Heights apartment, he and Betty rented a drafty efficiency attached to a farmhouse. When not teaching at Purdue, to keep midwestern boredom at bay, your future-father did pastel sketches of red barns and duck ponds, and wrote the first of his several never-to-be-published science fiction novels.[17]

Though he enjoyed certain aspects of it – the big skies, the rolling farmlands, the red dairy barns, the operatic lightning and snowstorms – Paul Selgin wasn't cut out for the Midwest. He found midwesterners narrow-minded and bland. He longed to return to the East Coast, to engineering and inventing. So when the offer came from the National Bureau of Standards in Washington, D.C., to be leader of a team in its Ordnance Development Division, to Betty's dismay, he jumped on it.

To his decision to have his mother join them in D.C., Betty responded, "Over my dead body."

Your future-father was adamant. Much as he may have resented her, he refused to leave his mother alone in New York.

---

[17]   I have three of my father's sci-fi novels. One, *The Twin Planet*, depicts an agrarian utopian Earth on which dominant Amazonia women suckle infant-sized males. This from a man who detested his overprotective mother.

He was, after all, still an Italian son, a *mammone*. He would not capitulate.

And so, while your future-father moved to Washington, D.C., with his mother, Betty and his daughters boarded a train bound for New York City. Days after arriving there she filed for a divorce.

The Bureau's Ordnance Development Division was charged with developing fuses for munitions – bombs, rockets, and mortar shells. As of that winter of 1943, its focus was the "proximity fuze," a fuze designed to detonate at the instant when the distance to a target fell short of a pre-determined length, resulting in greater accuracy and far more destruction.[18]

Though the proximity fuze helped the Allies win, and hence shortened, the war, your future-father could not have been pleased with his role in its development. Nor could the war's end have brought much relief, not after he learned of the annihilation of two Japanese cities by a pair of hydrogen bombs using an analogous detonation technology developed by another team of his division.

Still, your future-father kept his new job. In fact he was promoted to a higher position, one requiring greater security clearance. And so on the fifth day of February 1946, at the District Court in Brooklyn, New York, pursuant to Petition No. 414545, under the name Paul Joseph Selgin, your future-father became a U.S. citizen. Thus the last trace of Paolo Giuseppe Senigaglia was extinguished.

All Paul Selgin needed now was a family to carry on his new name.

WHILE WORKING AT the fuze lab (whose employees, incidentally, were forbidden to utter the word *bomb*), your future-father met Margaret, the American scientist who would become his second wife. At lunch, while she went about collecting dues for her union, he followed her around, until he screwed up the courage to speak to her. Following an eight-month courtship, he and Margaret

---

18   Today many consider it one of the most significant technological developments of World War II, bested only by radar and the atomic bomb. No less a figure than General Patton called the new fuze "devastating to the enemy" and credited it with winning the Battle of the Bulge.

married and bought a house together in Bethesda, one with extra rooms they would rent out, plus a spare room for his mother.

"I was extremely naïve," Margaret confessed in a letter she wrote you in answer to one you'd sent her. Not only was she completely unaware that her husband was Jewish, it had taken her two years into their marriage to learn that he was Italian.

"I asked him about his name," she wrote. "I'd never heard the name Selgin before, so I was curious. Anyway that's how I found out."

It was the Selgin name, ultimately, that ended your future-father's second marriage. He and Margaret had been vacationing together in Martha's Vineyard, renting bicycles and staying at a hostel there, when she confessed to him that as a result of an operation she'd had thirty years before she could not have children.

"Your father about fell apart," Margaret wrote. "He so wanted a son to carry on that clever name of his that he was so proud of. I wanted that as much for him as he did for himself. That's why I left him, one of the reasons."

"I still remember the day we parted," Margaret's letter continues. "He was behind the wheel of his yellow Studebaker. I stood next to the car, saying something about how maybe we should try again. 'It's a little late for that, isn't it?' he said, and then he drove away just like that. But I knew I'd made the right decision. He wanted a son to carry his name. I knew I couldn't deprive him of that."

That your father had been so eager for a male heir, that he'd taken such pride in his newly minted name, was puzzling to you, who never thought of your father as someone capable of pride, who considered him immune to that sentiment.

But the pride your future-father took in his name wasn't patriarchal or paternal. It was an artist's pride in his creation. He wanted his creation to survive him. He longed for a male heir. He got twice what he'd bargained for.

While vacationing in Italy, in the small hamlet of Bettola in the outskirts of Piacenza, your future-father met his third and final wife. Giuseppantonia DePoli was in every respect the antithesis of his first two wives. A dark beauty of twenty-six – fifteen years his junior – she spoke not a single word of English. Nor did she display much intellect, though she was witty and bright. He wooed her with his Charles Boyer good looks, his Renaissance genius, his worldly sophistication. Following a yearlong courtship via airmail, he returned to Italy to marry her. A few days after the wedding, he flew her back to the United State. There, nine months later, at Suburban Hospital in Bethesda, Maryland, at two o'clock on the morning of February 15, 1957, she gave birth to a pair of boys.

With his new wife, your father experienced another emotion of which you had never suspected him: jealousy. At the fancy Washington, D.C., parties, as your father looked on eagerly from across the room, packs of eligible bachelors and perfidious husbands alike were drawn like sharks to chum to Pinuccia Selgin's dark beauty.

His jealousy, along with his disgust with the bureau's bureaucracy and disillusionment with his role in what President Eisenhower dubbed the "Military Industrial Complex," prompted Paul J. Selgin to resign his position as head of the Electronics Division at the Washington Bureau of Standards, a post to which he had recently been promoted and for which he earned the then princely salary of forty-thousand dollars per year.

He had de bess job, your mother told you. An you papa, he trow it away – just like dat! – all to keep me away from dose udder men. He was very possessive, you papa.

Paul Selgin moved his new family to Bethel, a down-at-the-heels former hat-factory town in southwestern Connecticut, a place where his beautiful wife (who hadn't learned to drive and barely spoke English) was unlikely to encounter eligible males. In the converted barn of a black market farm there, he embarked on his new career as a freelance inventor.[19]

---

19   His first big project: the dollar-bill-changing machine for which he wouldn't "earn a nickel." The story of the ill-fated "Nomoscope" is told through a series of affidavits and letters to and from attorneys, and is much more complicated than my father's glum one-line party quip suggests. In 1958, two years after moving to Bethel, through a man by the name of Peter Treves (no relation to my father's family, I'm told), his patent attorney and business partner, an agreement was reached whereby the technology of my father's new invention was leased to the American Totalisator Company, which would mass produce and sell it. Within a year of that agreement, suddenly dollar bill changing machines began popping up in train stations and airline terminals

across the country–manufactured not by American Totalisator, but by two other firms: Universal Controls, Inc. and National Rejectors, Inc. There followed a rapid series of accusatory letters, claiming that Totalisator had, for a kickback, underhanded the technology to the other firms. To prove it, the machines had to be seized by court order, taken apart and examined by patent investigators. The case dragged on for a half-dozen years, ending with no proof and a settlement of $10,000–barely enough to cover legal costs for my father and his partner–who, it turned out, had himself for a hefty sum underhanded my father's invention to those two other companies. By the time he learned this, my father was so fed up with the whole megillah he refused to pursue it any further.

One day while vacationing in Venice during the summer of 2000, at a café where I'd been doing a watercolor, I met Michael Philip Davis, an opera singer and director, who subsequently invited Paulette and me over to his mother's palazzo for drinks. His mother, it turned out, was the famous diva Regina Resnik. Her palazzo was on the Giudecca. When we arrived we were shown to the balcony, where two women were seated. One of the women was Valerie Heller, *Catch-22* author Joseph Heller's recent widow; the other introduced herself as Vivian Treves.

"Your father wasn't by any chance an inventor?" she asked when she heard my name.

Though I resisted saying so, she was the daughter of Peter Treves, the man principally responsible for my father's never making a nickel from his Nomoscope.

MY MOTHER WAS INSTINCT AND EMOTION, MY FATHER *logic and intellect. If they ever shared a bed I never saw it. They fought terribly, Papa with reason on his side, my mother with passion and projectiles. One time she scrawled on the living room walls with a black grease pencil. She'd just finished painting the walls herself, dark purple, like the inside of a giant grape. The fight had been over that color. My mother asked my father what color she should paint the living room. "Why don't you paint it purple?" he'd said. He'd been joking, of course. But she didn't know it and went ahead and painted the room.*

We used to beg our parents to divorce, that's how bad their fights were. Though Mom threw things, she and my father never laid hands on each other. The blows were strictly verbal. Words were weapons. I can still hear my father's sneered "viles" and "loathsomes," his face burning red, saliva spraying from his lips. He fought in English; she Italian. Cretino. Maledetto. Vile. Loathsome. The words launched like mortars.

Reason and passion at war, twin children caught in the crossfire, ducking for cover.

It was my wish, my longing, to be loved by these very different people who barely understood each other, who – if they spoke at all to each other – used words as ordnance. Words were murderous, made to wound or be misunderstood. Is it any wonder I put my trust in pictures? In Mrs. Decker's kindergarten class, I drew fire engines, ocean liners, the Empire State Building lit up at night. Papa put the drawings into a file folder we called the "museum." With pictures, there was no question of being misunderstood.

In my worst dreams I'd try to make my parents understand me with words. One recurrent nightmare took place in the kitchen. I'd be trying to explain something to my mother and father, something important. My mother stirred something in a pot on her big black Chamber's stove; my father sat in the breakfast nook with his paper. They nodded their heads, or ignored me, but neither of them seemed to actually understand whatever it was that I was trying to explain to them. And so I raised my voice. I shouted. I screamed. Still, they either didn't seem to understand, or they ignored me. That's when I started breaking dishes. I opened the kitchen cupboard and threw one plate after another, hurling them onto the floor. All the while my mother stirred her Bolognese sauce and Papa read the paper as if I weren't there screaming and smashing plates.

I was in high school when I first had this dream.

The ability to understand each other through words is the thing that civilizes people, that keeps them from tearing each other apart. The war between my parents resulted directly from their failure to speak the same language. Though they both spoke Italian, my father spoke the language of reason and logic, while my mother spoke one of irony and innuendo. A picture may be worth a thousand words; a gesture may embody reams of psychology and philosophy. But the subtlest and most complex emotions demand nuances only spoken language can afford, and only if the language is shared.

My inventor Papa, working in his rat-hole laboratory at the base of our driveway, in turning a brass or aluminum shaft would adjust the bit of his lathe within a tolerance of one in ten thousand. I marveled at the precision of the adjustments by those hands darkened with metal grunge. I thought if I could calibrate my words with the same level of precision, within the same tolerance, then I might build something out of them that would assure me the understanding that I never achieved in that terrible dream; I could make myself heard without having to scream or smash plates. At long last, I'd be understood.

* * *

MY MOTHER'S BEAUTY. THE DRY, DUSTY LIBYAN CLIMATE. *The winds of the Sirocco blowing their dust over the Mediterranean,*

Malta, Italy, Croatia, Tunisia. The winds blow at a maximum speed of 100 kilometers an hour and are most prevalent during the autumn and the spring. The little girl in the yard of her villa, straddling a wall in the shade of a fig tree or her brother's Lambretta, spluttering down a palm tree-lined boulevard. Frozen in her eternal adolescence, in an endless flirtation with a world that ended, for her, on or around June 28, 1940, the day Italian anti-aircraft guns accidentally shot down Italo Balbo's Savoia-Marchetti in the skies over Tobruk. She was twelve years old and hasn't trusted anyone since. I want to write about her beauty, which has challenged, impressed, and annoyed me, the sudden vision of her naked at the top of the stairs from which, still a child, I was forced to shield my eyes. How she kept things hidden from me in secret drawers, and other things kept secret – the disparity between what she knew and what she was willing to disclose. For most of the time growing up I could not trust her. Words were articles of concealment. To utter a truth was to negate it; to speak (for her) was to lie. Sincerity existed in a realm beyond words, sacred and private, not to be shared, or anyway not to be confounded with language.

At eighty-seven my mother is still strikingly beautiful. From her I inherited my powers of charm and seduction.

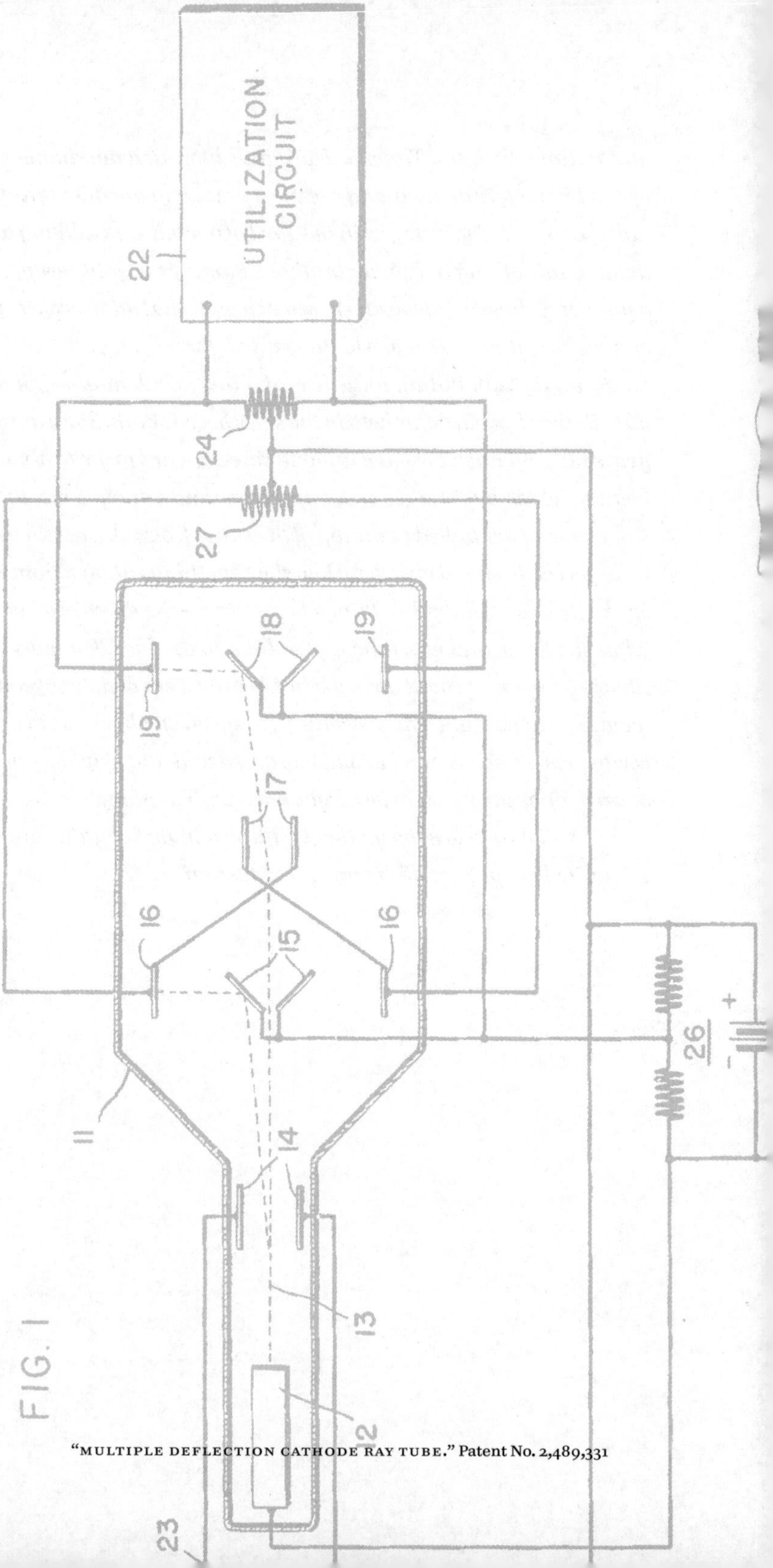

FIG. 1

"MULTIPLE DEFLECTION CATHODE RAY TUBE." Patent No. 2,489,331

XXVII.

Spuyten Duyvil, Bronx, New York, 2002

TWO YEARS AFTER YOUR FATHER DIED – TWENTY-THREE years after the teacher and you had last seen or spoken with each other – the teacher phoned you.

By then you and your wife were living in Spuyten Duyvil. In the early hours after midnight, in your studio during one of your frequent insomnia bouts, you googled the teacher's name. You'd never done so before, in part because you weren't sure what you would find or that you'd be ready to find it, but also because you wanted to (as you put it to yourself) "let sleeping dogs lie." Now, though, your curiosity exceeded your reluctance, and so you typed the teacher's name into the search field and hit "return" to find that the teacher was a full professor at a university in Oregon. More searching turned up a faculty directory with the teacher's name listed along with his office phone number.

Later that same day you tried the number to find it non-working. By then you were too curious to let it go at that. You phoned the university switchboard and asked for assistance. While waiting for the operator to direct your call you heard a call-waiting signal and switched to the other line. A gentle voice that you recognized instantly asked:

What are you doing?

I was calling directory assistance, you answered, laughing.

Well, you got direct assistance, said the teacher.

For the next hour you and the teacher spoke. You spoke of the things each of you had been up to since you last saw each other, you of earning a livelihood through painting and illustration, he of obtaining his doctoral degree and teaching classes at several programs at different universities before going on to co-found and head the Indigenous Studies Department at his present institution, working with Native Americans and refugees from Vietnam and Cambodia. He'd been to Vietnam many times, the teacher told you, and had even set up an exchange program with a university there, the first ever of its kind in that country. Like you, the teacher was married now, he explained, to a Vietnamese woman twelve years older than he. He spent about half his time with her in Vietnam, at her home in Da Lat.

She speaks no English, he explained. And she refuses to come to America.

Why is that?

She's afraid of airplanes.

You spoke of your own marriage, of your wife's and your struggles to make ends meet as artists, of minor victories and defeats. Though it was nearly noon, you were still wearing your bathrobe. Paulette was in some other part of the house, in her study or in the kitchen, reading or writing or cooking (she'd studied at the French Culinary Institute and become a proficient chef). She was at most a dozen yards away, yet she may as well have been on another planet in another galaxy, so unaware was she of the history being revisited in another room.

All this time while you spoke with the teacher you couldn't stop smiling, nor could you ignore the fact that the teacher and you were talking around something, namely that summer back in Corvallis twenty-three years ago. What had happened back then? What had gone wrong? Had there really been two hundred dollars in that box on the shelf behind your bed? Had Curtis really accused you of stealing it? Had the teacher and Curtis been lovers? Why had they treated you so coldly? The truth, that's all you wanted. You wanted to know the truth.

I've never stopped thinking of you, you said. All these years.

Same here, said the teacher.

I've missed you, you said. It was true. You'd missed him, or rather you missed the good parts of the past that you and he once shared together.

At last, during a lull in the conversation, you said:

What happened back then, that summer in Oregon?

What do you mean?

Curtis, the money I supposedly stole, how things ended between us.

Who says they ended?

You know what I mean.

It was a long time ago, Peter. I doubt I could remember many details if I tried. All I know is it wasn't a good time for us to be together. Our relationship had come to a turning point. It happens; things change. As transitions go, it wasn't very smooth. I wished it had come about more gently. I was sorry about that. I know you were very hurt. I know that you were bitter. I don't blame you. I was bitter myself, but for different reasons.

Why were you bitter?

I wasn't bitter toward you. I felt bitter toward myself.

Why?

For not having handled things differently, for not having handled them better. The fact is I didn't want to be your teacher anymore.

Who said I wanted you to go on being my teacher?

It wasn't a matter of what you wanted so much as of what you obviously needed. I just couldn't fill that role anymore.

You could have said so.

You're right, Peter, I could have. It might have spared you some suffering. It might have spared us both some pain. But I didn't. Maybe because I was angry at you for putting me a position where I had to choose between a friendship with you that came with the obligation to go on being someone I no longer was or wanted to be or sacrificing our friendship. I guess I made the latter choice. And who knows, maybe the suffering was necessary; maybe that's what it took.

What it took to what?

For us both to move on.

After a long pause you blurted: *Are you gay?*

Sounds of Henry Hudson Bridge traffic filled the ensuing silence.

I just told you I've been married for six years.

Yeah, I know, but –

Listen to me, Peter. When you and I first became friends thirty-three years ago, I told you people wouldn't be able to understand our friendship, what you and I had together. Remember? I tried to warn you back then that it was too special for most people to understand, that it wouldn't fit well into any of their recognizable categories, but that they were still bound to try and label it, the way you're trying to label it right now.

I'm sorry, you said. I don't want to label anything. I just had to ask.

Why? To know what? To put our friendship in a box? Is that really what you want, Peter, after all these years?

The teacher spoke gently, almost a whisper. Still you heard traces of anger and disappointment in his voice.

That's not what I wanted, you said.

Then why ask whether or not I'm gay?

I'm sorry. Your felt your cheeks flush with a thirteen-year-old's embarrassed disappointment in himself.

No need to be. For the millionth time there's not a box for what you and I had, Peter. If there were it wouldn't come with a convenient label.

The conversation went on for another half hour or so and ended politely, with you telling the teacher if he should ever find himself on the East Coast he should look you up, that Paulette and you would love to have him over. I know she'd like to meet you, you said. God knows I've talked enough about you to her! And she's a fabulous cook. She'll put out an amazing spread!

The teacher reciprocated, saying if you should ever come to Oregon you should do likewise. He didn't mean it, of course. Neither did you.

After you'd hung up, it occurred to you: you still had no idea who the teacher really was. You felt as if your world had just been painted some hopelessly ambiguous combination of drab shades, like camouflage.

You wished you hadn't spoken with him, that you'd let sleeping dogs lie.

A MONTH LATER you got another unexpected phone call, this one from Vivian. Since graduating from Bethel High you hadn't seen or heard from her, though you'd heard rumors that she moved to Boston, where she'd taken up with a professional ice hockey player.

Vivian tells you she's living in New York, where she's been involved in the theater, writing books and lyrics for musicals, including one about Hamlet's doomed sweetheart Ophelia (*"You know not what you've done / You should become a nun"*).

You meet at the Metropolitan – the museum, not the opera house. Having arrived early, you check your shoulder bag. You wear a pair of fresh black corduroy pants with a white turtleneck. You want to look your very best, to demonstrate that you have, so far, persevered if not prevailed in the battle against time and decay. Only after you've boarded the Metro North local to Grand Central does it occur to you that white turtlenecks had been one of the teacher's trademarks.

It's raining. You stand at the top of the stairs leading up to the museum entrance, holding an umbrella, watching people come and go, trying to imagine what Vivian will look like after so many years, picturing gray hair and the frowsy wardrobe of a woman past caring what strangers – men especially – think of her looks. All this time a slender woman with dark brown henna-colored hair stands holding her own umbrella at the bottom of the stairs, gazing at a mansion on the far side of Fifth Avenue. She wears a black dress with a bright Hermes scarf. Her left arm is perched on the brass railing.

Could it be?

You approach slowly and speak her name.

Vivian?

She turns, smiles. You hug, then you stand back to inspect each other. She hasn't changed, yet she has. Except for the artificially dark hair she looks like her younger self, but a synthetically preserved version of her younger self. Her face is thinner, her cheeks flatter. The little *Chickarina* meatball is still there, still clinging to the tip of her straight nose. When she smiles you notice that her teeth aren't in great shape (but, come to think of it, they never were). For a moment, that part of you that remains thirteen years old relishes her having made these small yet inevitable concessions toward decay and decrepitude, until it occurs to you that she's having similar thoughts about you.

Should we go to the café? you suggest.

YOU FIND A table by the enormous window. Low murmur of sophisticated voices, view of Central Park, rain sliding down huge panes. No cell phones permitted.

You make small talk. Careers, health, interests, relationships past and present. The musical Vivian mentioned on the phone is the only one she had any success with. Since then she hasn't been able to get so much as a reading of one of her plays at a decent theater. She walks dogs for a living.

Dogs shit a lot, Vivian informs you. But at least they don't make *me* feel like shit.

You share some of your own career woes, making them sound worse than they are.

When you've exhausted all other topics, Vivian says:

Would you like to talk about——? She invokes the teacher's name.

Sure, you say. Why not? (It's all you've been wanting to do, really.)

She tells you she last saw him when she was eighteen, a little over a year after she graduated from high school, when "suddenly, out of the blue," in the mail she received from him what she describes as a "very intense letter; a passionate letter."

Very passionate, she repeats.

Had he written to you before that?

Vivian shakes her head. Not that it mattered. His letter made it clear that he hadn't forgotten about me, that I'd been on his mind ever since he left Bethel.

You give Vivian a puzzled look.

Let's just say it was a very romantic letter, she says.

Romantic? you say.

It was a love letter, she admits finally with a sigh. He confessed his love to me. He was living in Boston at the time. You know he lived in Boston?

Yeah. He wrote me from there, you say. A couple times.

Did he? (This doesn't seem to please her.)

By then I'd been accepted by the Boston Conservatory, Vivian goes on. A coincidence? Fate? Who knows. Back then I used to think everything was fate ... Anyway, I went to visit him there. In Boston. I rode the bus. He had an apartment by the Fenway. I think he may have been living with some guy, I'm not sure. Anyway, I had his letter to me tucked in my purse. I must have read it fifty times on the damn Greyhound bus. He met me at the terminal. We went out to dinner, a steakhouse. He seemed – nervous. All through the meal he kept fidgeting, looking at his watch. I asked if anything was wrong. The third time I asked him, he snapped at me. *Why do you keep asking that?* I said since you keep fidgeting and looking at your damn watch. He said that lately he'd been under a lot of pressure. I forget the reason or reasons he gave. To be honest, I don't remember all that much about that evening, except that he was obviously very nervous and things didn't go very well. They didn't go well at all.

Doesn't sound like you had a good time, you remark.

He treated me like I was still his student – like I was still in eighth grade, like five years hadn't happened. He didn't seem able to deal with the fact that in the meantime I'd become a full-grown woman. He seemed to want to ignore that little fact, or deny it, as if the grown-up me wasn't sitting right there in front of him, as if he was having dinner with some fourteen-year-old girl, someone he didn't have to take quite so seriously, at least not romantically, anyway. It was one of the worst nights of my life. No, scratch that. It was *the* worst night of my life.

You wait for her to say more.

That's it, she says. We said goodbye and I rode the Greyhound back home.

You never saw him again?

Vivian shakes her head. Nope. Never, she says.

After a pause she adds: I'm still recovering.

AFTER LEAVING THE museum, in a downpour, Vivian and you walk to the subway entrance. On the way there she says:

I was almost afraid to call you. I wasn't sure that you'd want to hear from me again after how I treated you back in high school. If my memory serves me I was pretty damn shitty to you.

I won't disagree, you say.

I was a mean fucking bitch.

If you want an argument you won't get one from me.

If it's not too late, I'd like to apologize. She says this without looking at you and as the rain falls harder. You both step over an overflowing gutter.

There's nothing to apologize for. You were young. We were both young. And if *my* memory serves me, I was a pretty big jerk myself.

Well, I'm sorry if I was cruel. It wasn't called for.

At the subway entrance, you both collapse your umbrellas. Vivian kisses you on the cheek and rushes down the stairs to the subway. You're both headed the same direction, downtown to Grand Central, but from the way she hurries down those stairs it's clear to you that she's had enough of your company. You'll never see or hear from her again.

* * *

FOUR YEARS LATER, ANOTHER INSOMNIA-INSPIRED WEE hour web search produced the teacher's obituary. Of course you were stunned. For a long time you sat there, staring at the headline before even clicking on the newspaper article. It seemed impossible to you – not so much because the teacher died so young (he was only sixty-three), but because through all these years somewhere in the back of your mind you still believed the day would arrive when you and he would be united again. Though consciously you had relinquished that hope, dismissed and outgrown and even found it objectionable, deep inside, instinctively, even as you approached your forty-seventh birthday, you continued to cling to it.

According to the obituary, the teacher's family had chosen not to specify the cause of death, though "a history of heart problems" was alluded to. Apart from the teacher's untimely death itself, several things about the notice that ran in a local Oregon newspaper struck you as curious, and not just curious, but alarming.

The obituary stated that the teacher had been "a member of the Seneca Tribe of Indians." This was news to you. The teacher had never said anything to you about having Native American origins, let alone being a member of any tribe.

The notice went on to say that, according to his sister, the teacher attended what at the time was a community college in Connecticut. It made no mention of the teacher's having been a Rhodes Scholar and gone to Oxford and Berkeley. Nor did the obituary mention the fact that he'd been adopted. It said only that he had been survived by two sisters and a brother. Yet you could have sworn – in fact you were certain – that when you knew him the teacher told you he was adopted, that he'd never known his biological parents, and furthermore that one of his adoptive brothers, a paraplegic, the Man in the Wheelchair, had abused him.

For a moment you wondered if possibly the obituary was that of a different person with the same name. But no: it was the teacher, there was no question about it. Further searches on the internet turned up other articles published on the occasion of the teacher's death, including one accompanied by a photograph of the teacher standing at a podium behind a microphone, wearing the bone pendant and Indian-pattered vest, his formerly blond hair dyed black and worn in a ponytail under a khaki baseball cap.

Not long afterward you discovered the obituary of the young

man the teacher had been living with when you visited him in Oregon. Curtis. He died less than a month after the teacher, the cause of death undisclosed.

What had caused Curtis's death? And the teacher's? Had they been lovers? Had the teacher been gay? Was he really Native American? Had he gone to Oxford? Or had he lied about those and other things? If he lied, why did he lie? For what reason? To what end? Who was the teacher? Who had he been, really? And why did it matter?

Did it matter?

It did. It mattered to you because your idea of yourself, your identity, was built in large measure on the belief that you were special, and this belief, this notion, had been underwritten if not occasioned outright by your friendship with the teacher, by his having taken you into his confidence and made you his friend. And though that friendship had come to a pathetic end, in spite of its ending, still, you'd held on to that fundamental belief; you had clung to it. And now the identity of the human being who had been its basis – the keystone in the archway of your ego – had come under question. Therefore you had to know. Your own identity depended on it.

And so, as you had done with your father six years before, you set out to learn all that you could about the teacher.

IN THE WIDELY HELD VIEW OF CONTEMPORARY PSY-
*chologists, each of us, to a greater or lesser extent, erects a so-called
"false self." Whereas a person's real or true self is rooted in the primary
experience of being alive, of lungs breathing and heart beating and
blood pumping through veins, the false self has its origins in the expec-
tations of others, it's the defensive façade we construct to protect ourselves from encroachments from without – initially from the demands
and wishes of our parents, but also from the demands imposed on us
subsequently by others. To the extent that we feel that others don't
care enough about us, our needs and our feelings, that we don't matter, that who and what we essentially are is somehow insufficient to
earn a sense of belonging, then we create a false sense in order to gain
back that sense.*

*In the long run, the false self originating out of a childhood need
to connect may become like a drug to which we become addicted, so
being "special" becomes the only way to live, and living as a false self
becomes the only way to feel special.*

*The strain of maintaining such a false identity often leads to
depression and anxiety later on in life. It also inhibits or precludes the
possibility of developing one's true self and authentic personality, of
achieving, in Maslow's term, self-actualization. ...*

*We know also from Jung, and from our earlier discussion of psycho-
logical polarities, that conscious and unconscious are riven into that
strife of father and son, or of ego and Self, by the ego which either*

"father" or "son" may dominate and whose dividing light makes differences in our wholeness.

Pathological lying (PL) is characterized by a long history (maybe lifelong) of frequent and repeated lying for which no apparent psychological or external benefit can be discerned.

> JAMES HILLMAN, *"Sinex and Peur: An Aspect of the Historical and Psychological Present."*

Ethnic fraud: *falsely claiming American Indian heritage or other minority status in order to boost job prospects. (See Ward Churchill, Andrea Smith, and most recently Rachel Dolezal.)*

In the end, perhaps Dolezal simply believed the convictions of her academic culture a little too much. After all, we on the left have insisted for years that the various demographic categories we are placed into are merely social constructs, the creation of human assumption and human prejudice. That race is a social construct is a stance that brooks no disagreement in left-wing spaces.

> FREDRIK DEBOER, *"Why Rachel Dolezal would want to pass as a black woman,"* L.A. Times *op-ed.*

The daughter of Sky Woman gave birth to twins. Right-Handed Twin was born the normal way. Left-Handed Twin forced himself out of his mother's left armpit, killing her ...

Together the twins invented the world. Right-Handed Twin created mountains, lakes, blossoms, gentle creatures; Left-Handed Twin created cliffs, whirlpools, thorns, thunder, and predators. Right-Handed Twin was truthful, reasonable, goodhearted, and honest; Left-Handed Twin lied, fought, rebelled, and made questionable choices ...

The Iroquois believe that Left-Handed Twin and Right-Handed Twin are both necessary for the world to be in balance.

IROQUOIS CREATION MYTH

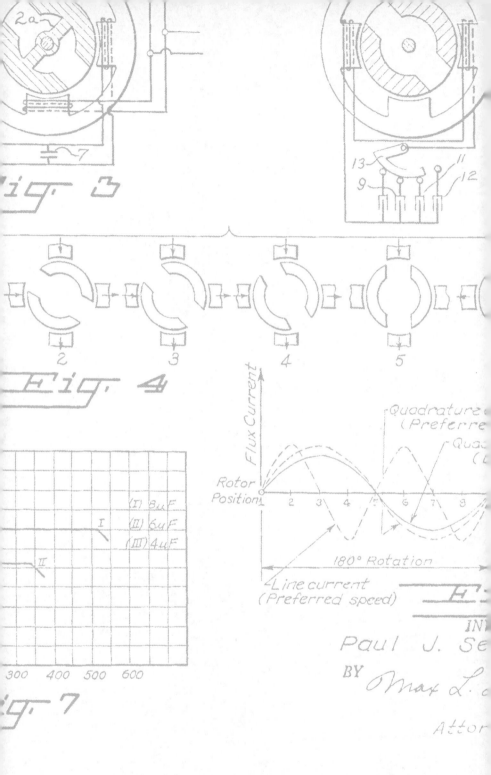

"INDUCED QUADRATURE FIELD MOTOR." From Patent No. 2,736,853

XXVIII.

Castalia

1943 – 2006

YOU PORED THROUGH ARTICLES AND WEBSITES. YOU found a newspaper article published almost ten years before the teacher's death. It emphasized the teacher's ties, not to his ancestral tribal roots, but to Vietnam, to where he was about to journey for the ninth time in connection with the exchange program he had helped establish there.

According to the article, the teacher's ties with Vietnam stretched back across fifty years, to World War II, when his father had been part of an army team assigned to help Ho Chi Minh fight the Japanese. According to the article, *three* of the teacher's brothers had fought in the Vietnam War.

"One lost his life," said the article, "another his legs, the third his place is society; he couldn't relate to people anymore." Later, when the teacher was a graduate student, as refugees from Southeast Asia began pouring into the United States, their struggle to assimilate into a foreign culture affected him deeply "because of his own American heritage" – a statement that, if it pointed at all to the teacher's indigenous roots, did so ambiguously at best.

Otherwise the article said nothing about the teacher's origins, tribal or otherwise. It focused instead on the enormous changes Vietnam had undergone since the war, on the reestablishment of diplomatic and other relations between it and the United States, and on the teacher's "enchantment" with those changes.

"My one regret," the article concludes with the teacher saying, "is that my brothers aren't alive to see it."

YOU WROTE A letter to the teacher's one surviving relative, his sister, a brief note to which you appended your phone number and the wish that she get in touch with you. "It would mean a lot to me," you wrote.

A few days after you posted the letter, the teacher's sister phoned you.

What would you like to know? she asked.

She had a husky voice.

Through the teacher's only surviving sibling, you learned that he never went to Oxford. He never went to Berkeley. He'd had seven siblings, including two brothers, each of who served in Vietnam. One brother was killed in action there, the other suffered permanent mental wounds. Yes, there'd been a third brother who was a paraplegic, but he hadn't been injured in the war; he had indeed broken his spine jumping off a bridge into a lake. His name was Frank. He might have abused his younger brother, it was possible, she couldn't say for sure.

Your brother told me he was adopted. Was he?

Is that what he said? She laughed. That doesn't surprise me.

Not true?

No, but I understand why he said it.

Their family had been "dirt poor," nine of them living in a four-room double-wide house infested with mice and cockroaches. Their father had been a drunk unemployed firehose factory worker with emphysema. They survived on welfare and food stamps.

What else do you want to know? the teacher's sister asked you.

Are you Native American?

Oh that, the teacher's sister said. There may be some native blood on my mother's side. She used to talk about it. There were stories. That's all I can tell you.

From his surviving sister you'll learn that, during the last months of the teacher's life, when he and Curtis both knew he was dying, Curtis took to drinking heavily.

Yes, she said, anticipating your next question. Curtis committed suicide.

Were he and your brother lovers?

I really don't know. Let's just say their relationship was very intense.

Was your brother married?

Not that I know of.

He told me he had a wife in Vietnam.

Did he? That's the first I've heard of it.

He said he lived with her six months out of the year.

News to me.

Was he lying, do you think?

With my brother anything was possible. He traveled to Vietnam a lot. He was close to a lot of people there. Maybe he married one of them. Who knows?

What else can I tell you? the teacher's surviving sister said as your phone conversation drew to its close. He was a good man, my brother, a very good man. He truly wanted to help people. He did help them, hundreds of them. He died helping them. In the last half-dozen years of his life, he made something like forty trips to Vietnam and back. His weak heart couldn't take it anymore. He broke it helping other people. He broke Curtis's heart, too. And just about everyone that knew and loved him. Mine especially. He broke my heart. I'm still trying to recover. No – I take that back. I won't ever recover. He was very dear to me. He was by far my favorite brother. I still can't believe he's gone.

And you? the teacher's sister asked you after a pause. Why does any of this matter so much to you? Who was my brother to you?

It was what you were trying to figure out.

We were friends, you answered. Close friends.

THE NEXT ITEM of evidence you uncovered was a video interview produced by the cable channel of the university where the teacher had worked at the time of his death. The interview was conducted by an attractive, if nervous-looking, young woman with a pageboy hairdo. She introduced the teacher, listing his many accomplishments as a champion of indigenous peoples and their causes, how he had planned and organized schools, launched exchange programs, and had been instrumental in forming and strengthening global alliances between universities and other institutions in Vietnam and elsewhere.

To one of her questions the teacher responds: *The challenge isn't merely for indigenous and other culturally displaced people and immigrants to enjoy the rights of other established citizens but to hold onto their history – to where they come from and what makes them distinct. I don't subscribe to the melting-pot metaphor. You shouldn't have to melt. You shouldn't have to give up your cultural roots to be part of a new culture.*

As in the photograph in one of the obituaries, the teacher wears his dyed hair in a ponytail under a khaki baseball cap. He still wears the round, metal-framed glasses he wore when you were his eighth-grade pupil.

Three-quarters of the way through the video the interviewer asks the teacher if he has a "personal stake in these challenges." There follows a lengthy pause during which the teacher casts his eyes upward. He licks his lips and blinks rapidly before saying:

That's a difficult question.

You don't have to answer it, the interviewer says.

No, no: let me see if I can do this …

The teacher explains that he comes from a mixed cultural background, that on his mother's side they were descended from the Six Nations of Seneca, otherwise known as the Iroquois by the French and by other names coined for them by their invaders. On his father's side they were Onondaga and Welsh. His father's family left Wales to work the coal mines of New York and northeastern Pennsylvania. Because miners were frowned upon by the earlier settlers, they were considered unsuitable material for marriage. Having few options, they'd often marry into native communities. *That's how the Onondaga and Seneca heritages were joined,* the teacher explains, adding: *But I consider myself a contemporary North American by destiny as well as by choice.*

The teacher's answers to the interviewer's questions seemed sincere, they sounded authentic. And anyway why would anyone make up such things – and in such great specific detail? Still, you were perplexed by the fact that in the time you knew him not once had the teacher mentioned any of these things to you. On the contrary, the things he did say contradicted them.

In the video the teacher goes on to explain how as a teenager he suffered an identity crisis, wondering who he was, where he belonged, and if he belonged anywhere. *Was I Onondaga? Welch? American?* He traveled to Wales, he explained, where he took part in an ancient druidic ceremony commemorating the onset of spring in which a seventy-foot-tall effigy of the Welch spring goddess Blodeuwedd sculpted from holly branches was set aflame and plunged into the Irish Sea.

Not the sort of thing I expected from white people, the teacher told the interviewer.

Though you spent the better part of the next hour trying, you were unable to verify whether such a ritual or anything like it had ever taken place in Wales, or, for that matter, anywhere else.

THAT FALL, YOU wrote to the Vital Records Specialist at the Allegany Clerk's Office of the Seneca Nation of Indians asking for any information they might have regarding the teacher's tribal heritage. Four months later, you received the following reply:

> Dear Mr. Selgin,
>
> This letter is in regards to a genealogy request that was received in this office on October 9, 2012, with respect to Mr. ———, born on April 16, 1943. Unfortunately, after an extensive search, I am unable to confirm any Seneca ancestry.
>
> Our census books contain only the names of Senecas that were residing on the Allegany Indian Reservation or the Cattaraugus Indian Reservation from 1858 through the late 1960s. The need for a census to be conducted was no longer required once the Tribal Roll System was established. Your relatives may very well have been of Seneca descent, but if they did not reside on the reservation during the census era, we would have no record of them.
>
> At this point my record will be filed as completed.

In a handwritten note accompanying the letter, the Vital Records Specialist notes that the teacher's surname "never existed in [their] census books or in the tribal roll."

STILL, YOU WEREN'T satisfied. Supposing the teacher never claimed he was "a member of the Seneca Nation of Indians"? What if the obituary had gotten things wrong? Obituaries are seldom written by their subjects, after all.

You watched the video interview again, this time with a notebook and pen in hand. Nowhere in it did the teacher say he was a member of the Seneca Nation. What he says is that his family *were descended from the Six Nations of Seneca.*

Also known as the Six Nations of the Grand River or the "Iroquois" Nation or Confederacy, the Six Nations of Seneca was a gathering of six culturally and linguistically similar native tribes that united to promote peace and harmony among themselves.[20]

The nation's existence dates back to the fifteenth century, when it occupied vast stretches of what is now New York State west of the Hudson, from the St. Lawrence River all the way down into northwest Pennsylvania. The term *Iroquois* having derived from a French mispronunciation of a derogatory expression used to describe them by their enemies, the nation's members prefer to call themselves *Haudenosaunee,* meaning "The People of the Longhouse," referring to the very large, very long, single-roomed dwellings erected for meetings and other communal functions.

Framed with sharp, fire-hardened poles driven close together into the ground, sided with strips of horizontally woven bark, and roofed with leaves and grasses, with flaps of animal hide covering their entryways to preserve warmth, the huts were typically fifteen to thirty feet wide and up to three hundred feet long, and roomy enough to house twenty or more families. They featured centrally located hearths for heating, cooking, and light, with holes above them that let out the smoke (and let in the snow and the rain).

---

20   In no special order the six tribes are:
       Mohawk (*Kanienkahagen*): "The People of the Flint"
       Oneida (*Onayotekaono*): "The People of the Upright Stone"
       Onondaga (*Onundagaono*): "The People of the Hills"
       Cayuga (*Guyohkohnyoh*): "The People of the Great Swamp"
       Seneca (*Onondowahgah*): "The People of the Great Hill"
       Tuscarora (*Ska-Ruh-Reh*): "The Shirt-Wearing People"

Apart from the practical purposes they served, the long-houses served an important symbolic function as well. They symbolized the traditions of their society, the nations that had bonded together to form their confederacy, with the Senecas the "Keepers of the Western Door," and the Mohawks the "Keepers of the Eastern Door," and the Onondagas the "Keepers of the Central Council Fire and Wampum." The longhouse was and remains to this day a powerful symbol of these ancient unions, of the members of different tribes coming together in peace and faith for the common good. *A place for people who still know how to think and dream.*

That the teacher was not a recognized member of the Seneca Nation of Indians did not preclude his having blood ties to any of the other five Haudenosaunee tribes, though proving this one way or another was impossible, since to your knowledge anyway none of the other tribes kept official records or membership roles.

Hence to the question: *Was the teacher a Native American?* you would never get a satisfactory, let alone a conclusive, answer. All you could be sure of was that the teacher had wanted an identity and heritage other than that imposed on him by his immediate background, by the environment of his birth. How strange, you thought, that this man so passionately devoted to helping other people hold onto or regain their cultural identities had been so unwilling to admit to himself or others where he'd really come from and who he really was.

It was strange, too, that the two men who had meant so much to you – your father and the teacher – both felt the need to break with their pasts and reinvent themselves.

Hadn't you done as much? Hadn't you likewise felt that same need to be someone else, namely someone other than your brother's twin? Hadn't you struggled to redefine yourself in the image of some ideal paradigm, the knight-errant in quest of the Holy Grail of an ideal father? Hadn't all your muddled struggles and wastrel wanderings boiled down to that otiose imperative? Were you not still, as a middle-aged man, conflicted regarding the sources of your own identity, wondering who your father – or fathers – were?

You lived, you loved, you had good friends and a good wife, a home and a career – all the trappings, in short, of a self-actualized existence, of a successful life. Yet under it all was the feeling that something wasn't quite right, that you'd never really grown, that the house of your self had been erected on a foundation of quicksand, or none at all. Not that you didn't know who you were, exactly, but that you doubted it.

Were you not still searching for that Holy Grail? Were you not, in other words, still searching for your god?

Aren't we all, always, by some means or other, searching for our inventors?

* * *

THERE WAS ONE OTHER PERSON YOU WANTED TO INTER-view. You phoned your mother.

Oh, he was *omosessual*, she said.

How do you know?

Because – he tell me!

Why would he tell you that?

I ask him. Dat time when he come for Christmas. After you go to bed, I ask. I say I like you very much, but is someting I need to ask you, an please no get mad at me. Dat when I ask him and when he tell me.

He said he was *gay?*

Your mother made a tsking sound. He no say gay, Peter!

What did he say?

I ask him are you omosessual an e say yes, Pinuccia. I say to eem I no give a goop if you omosessual. I know you a good man, I tell him, but I Peter mudder an I swear on god if you put a finger on my son I keel you.

Before getting off the phone with her you had one more question for your mother.

Does the name Bernice Mundt mean anything to you?

Who?

She came to Papa's funeral service. A German woman. Bernice. *Beh-reh-nee-chay.*

Ma va! Quella stronzo! She had de nerve to come to his funeral!

She told me Papa was Jewish.

Silence at your mother's end of the line.

Who is – or was – she?

One of you fadder girl friend. You know you Papa. My first
date in America he take me to dinner at de home of one of his girlfriend. She made chicken tetrazzini.

That was Berenice?

No, she was a different one. She live in New York. He go to
see her when he went der. I knew all about. I no stoopid. She call
him all de time at de house. I always knew was her; I could tell by
de way he talk. One day she call and I answer. She say, "Who are
you?" I say, "If you so interested in my husband, go ahead, you can
have him. I'm ready to divorce him." Den I trow down de phone.
Per l'amor di dio. After dat she never call again. I can't believe she
come to his funeral! *Cretino!*

Then, after a pause: Was good looking?

Nothing like you. She was German.

Figurati. He always like de German one. Probably a *furbacchi-
ona.* Papa like brain more den body. Why he marry me I never know.

Did you know Papa was Jewish?

No when I agree to marry him.

But you did know – eventually?

When I marry his cousin.

You married Papa's *cousin?*

You fadder couldn't come to Italy. He couldn't leave his work,
so to make thing go faster I marry his cousin by proxy. Later he come
to Italy an we get marry by de church. By den I knew was Jewish.

How did you know?

Because his cousin *look* Jewish. But by den was too late.

You'd have changed your mind because he was Jewish?

Dey took everything from us. During the war. Dey gave my
father forty-eight hour to leave Africa. Because he was antifascist.

He had to sell everything. Two Jewish men dey buy everything. In the beginning dey pay every month, but when the English take over dey stop. My family never see another penny. After the war my fadder try to find them, to get our money. Even Interpol could no find them. I still remember der name, Piccolo an Letizia. From den on I no like Jewish people.

Mom, don't say that!

Why no?

Because – it's terrible!

What can I say? Was a disaster.

For all you know those two men were exterminated! They probably ended up in a concentration camp. No wonder Interpol couldn't find them!

I was tirteen. You no forget ting dat happen when you tirteen.

So you knew all along about Papa?

I knew.

Why didn't you tell us?

I try to keep secret. I no want you and George to know.

Why not?

I no want you to be Jewish!

* * *

IN *THE FUTURE OF NOSTALGIA,* SVETLANA BOYM DEFINES nostalgia as "a longing for a home that no longer exists or has never existed." She distinguishes between two types of nostalgia: *restorative* and *reflective*. Reflective nostalgia thrives on the wistful longing for the past itself rather than on its attainment or recreation. Restorative nostalgia goes beyond mere longing to attempt an actual reconstruction of a lost, non-existent past.

"Reflective nostalgia," writes Boym, "dwells on the ambivalences of human longing." It cherishes the details of memory rather than its symbols. In so doing it calls into doubt any absolute truth about the past, leaving room for poetry, irony, and humor.

Restorative nostalgia, on the other hand, supports and protects an absolute utopian ideal of the past. "It takes itself dead seriously," Boym writes. According to Boym the restorative nostalgic knows two main plots: "the return to origins and the conspiracy." He seeks to turn history into a private or collective mythology.

* * *

THREE YEARS AFTER THE TEACHER'S DEATH YOU FOUND this newspaper item posted online:

UNIVERSITY OPENS
AMERICAN INDIAN LONGHOUSE

————, Oregon (AP), 2009. Two years after the death of the professor who conceived it, ———— has opened an American Indian longhouse, a community center traditional to many Native American peoples in the Pacific Northwest and around the country.

The 3,000-square-foot building stands as a symbol of two generations of effort, project leaders said.

"I can't help but be overwhelmed just to see the structure, to see all the new faces and all the old faces," said one recent doctoral graduate who was among those who helped see the longhouse project to completion.

"It's a place where people will achieve their academic dreams but also a place where spirit and community reside," the recent graduate said. "There's no limit to what can take place here."

The project is part of a program initiated under the former professor for whom a community of kindred souls had been a long-time dream.

The professor died in 2006.

American Indians remain the smallest ethnic minority and have the lowest college attendance rate of any racial group in the country.

Opening ceremonies for the Many Nations Longhouse included remarks from tribal elders as well as testimonials in honor of the project's originator. More events are planned for the building's inaugural year.

Castalia, the teacher's dream of a special community where scholars, teachers, and artists, *people who still know how to think and dream,* would come together, the dream that had been your dream too, had at long last come true.

Why do I write? To get out of hell.
ARTAUD

* * *

LET'S SAY THAT AT THE "TENDER AGE" OF THIRTEEN I *was seduced into an inappropriate relationship with the compassionate, complicated, lonely and confused man who was my eighth-grade English teacher. If so, that seduction was mutual. After all, I was its instigator.*

Yes, yes: I know: I was a boy and he was a grown man. Though it may have been mutual, the relationship was hardly equal.

Equal or not, my seductive skills were not something to be sneezed at. Still it was up to the teacher – the adult – to resist them.

In that case let's just agree that he had his work cut out for him.

* * *

INTERESTING HOW LIKE CERTAIN TWINS THE TEACHER *and my father mirror each other, with each having tried to redefine himself while escaping his past, but in opposite (and apposite) ways. For the teacher, the means to escape his immediate and embarrassing past was to embrace another past, one beyond the grasp of memory – a distant tribal heritage to which he made dubious if heartfelt claim. Whereas, regarding his past, my father adopted a scorched-earth policy, destroying anything that might have been useful to the enemy, the enemy being history, or rather the history imposed upon him by blood. Where the teacher chose to reconnect with what he believed to be his ancestral tribe, my father wanted no part of tribes of any kind, his own or anyone else's.*

The teacher's Castalia, his longhouse, was a communal structure, a place of sharing and learning, of diverse peoples and nations coming together as one. My father's Castalia – his paradise – was the rat-infested, rotted-floored Building in which he labored in blissful, fart-and-orange-rind-scented solitude, on his inventions.

* * *

I DREAM OF MY FATHER.

In the dream he sits smoking on the rooftop of a building. He looks about twenty-five and wears a white T-shirt. The building is a brownstone of the kind seen in Brooklyn or Hoboken. That's it, that's the whole dream. He just sits there, the man who will one day be my father, looking young and smoking. Out of such delicate dreams is the myth of my father constructed.

FOURTEEN YEARS HAVE passed since my father died. Now I'm a father myself. Audrey has just turned five.

On our visits together, Audrey and I have our rituals. When it's time for us to brush our teeth, we do it together, she with her baby toothbrush, I with my electric Braun. We stand facing each other in front of the bathroom sink, each with a hand on the counter, crossing our legs, she with left crossed over right, mine crossed the opposite way.

In other ways, too, Audrey and I mirror each other. She has my eyes – large, dark, round – and my mouth and stubby fingers. Her stubbornness, her cheeky humor, her rebellious insistence on having things her way – all these qualities reflect me, as I reflected the same qualities in my father and in the teacher.

Though written to my past self, really this book and its memories are for her. Until someone takes them from her, she'll carry these memories with her into the future. She'll be their custodian, the torchbearer of her father's myth, the exponent of this inventor and his inventions.

Dear beloved daughter, may this book be the bridge between my past and your future. May it help you invent your own memories, your own myths, your own dreams and desires.

May it help you invent yourself.

Afterword
George Selgin

"I'D LIKE YOU TO WRITE AN AFTERWORD FOR *THE INVENTORS.*"

You want me to do *what*?

"Write an afterword. You know, like an introduction, but at the end of the book."

I know what an afterword is. But why are you asking me? Who cares what I have to say about your book? Why not get someone famous to write it? No one is going to read your book because your brother says something nice about it. You might as well ask Mom to write something. Seriously. Ask your publisher.

"Actually, she's the one who suggested having you do it."

Then you have a crazy publisher.

"Actually, she seems very reasonable. And she knows what she's doing."

Let's hope so. But suppose I do write it. What do you expect me to say? If you think I'm going to tell everyone that it's all true, you can forget it. Remember how you asked me if I minded your including that crap about the fountain pen in your book of short stories? The one that got the whatchyamacallit prize? What was I supposed to do, tell you not to publish the damn thing so the world wouldn't think I was a big jerk? So I said go ahead, but how about writing something nice about me to make up for it? And you said you would. Remember? Well instead you've gone and repeated that same bullshit story again! So if you're thinking you can get me to swear it's all true you've got another…

"You don't have to say that the book is true. You can say whatever you want."

Do you really mean that?

"I do."

Okay, Peter. In that case, I'll do it. But I hope you know what
you're doing.

* * *

LET ME SET the record straight. Back in the summer of '78, I
wasn't getting a degree from Auburn University. I was only there
to take a few summer classes. And I lived in an apartment, not a
"dorm." Finally, although my brother visited me, I did not send him
packing for stealing a fountain pen from my "collection."

First of all, I don't like fountain pens. They leak. And the nibs
scratch the paper. Anyway, I never used them. And I certainly never
collected them. When Peter and I were just twenty-one, I was in
no position to collect anything. I had no money. My apartment in
Auburn was barely big enough for the palmetto bugs I had to share
it with. I lived on peanut butter sandwiches and, when I was feeling health-conscious, on raw broccoli dipped in Gulden's mustard.
(Like Wagner's music, it's better than it sounds.) Although I was
into bike racing – I spent my weekends that summer training or racing with Alabama's road-racing champ – I couldn't afford new tubu-
lar tires and had to patch and resew my flats. In short, if I had one
of anything, I considered myself lucky. If Peter stole any sort of pen
from me, it was almost certainly the only decent pen that I owned.

Would Peter have been capable of stealing his twin brother's
only pen? You bet! If anything, he was even poorer than me, and
he couldn't go a minute without scribbling something in his big
journal. But if he did, I don't remember. Nor do I remember having an argument with him, or telling him to get lost. I have a lousy
memory, so it's possible these things all happened. But I'm sure
there was no fountain pen.

I'm also pretty certain that I never called Peter a "libertine."
How come? Because even in 1978 I knew that "libertine" wasn't a

word one used to describe a pen thief. So I wouldn't have called Peter a libertine. If I called him anything, chances are I called him an asshole. I called him that all the time. I still call him that sometimes.

So much for the fountain-pen story. But that's just the tip of the iceberg–the George of *The Inventors* differs from the one I happen to be familiar with in lots of other ways. I'm telling you so not because you should care what I was or wasn't like but because this is one subject of *The Inventors* concerning which I can claim to be something of an authority. The George I recall was not especially fond of hot fudge sundaes (at Friendly's, he preferred the mint chocolate-chip ice cream, two scoops, best enjoyed while Peter and the other suckers were cramming for some test). He never earned a master's degree, from Duke or from anywhere else. Nor did he ever rig up a Bunsen burner to make it spew water, though he certainly would have done that had it been possible. His father never made him vomit, in a Chinese restaurant or anywhere else (though his mother did, once, by insisting that he finish his broccoli). And his sadistic ex-Navy SEAL scuba-diving instructor forced him to breathe, not from a valve-less tank–which was impossible–but from a regulator-less tank–which was possible, but only by breathing water along with one's air. Finally, the George I know did not lose his vir–

...Well, you get the idea. My brother, if not exactly a liar, can't be taken at his word.

Does this sort of thing make *The Inventors* phony? Supposing it did, so what? Plenty of famous memoirists have taken great liberties with the truth. And the most self-avowedly candid ones have tended to take the biggest liberties of all. Look at St. Augustine. Or Rousseau.

But *The Inventors* isn't phony in the sense of pretending to be anything other than what it is. Peter never claims that it's entirely candid or accurate. On the contrary, he warns his readers again and again against assuming that he is merely telling the truth. His book's title is itself a warning. It is a book about inventors whose inventions consist of myths they've spun about themselves. It is, most obviously, a book about two inventors: our father and our eighth-grade English teacher. But it is mostly about a third inventor, Peter himself, and his own creations, whose patent specification you are holding.

Since he asked me to write this afterword, Peter has also been pestering me to tell him what I think of *The Inventors*. I have not answered him, but now that I've said as much as I have about the book, I'm prepared to do so. *The Inventors* is at times beautiful and at others exasperating. It has brought back to me wonderful memories and also very sad ones. It has made me want to fling parts of it across the room and to read others again and again. It is to me, in short, everything that my brother himself is to me.

Do I like *The Inventors*? Of course not. I love it.

Acknowledgements

THANKS TO THE FOLLOWING PEOPLE:

Walter Cummins, Kate St. Ives, Sarah Krahulik Lenz, Sandra Worsham, Peter Nichols, Fred Eberstadt, Ed Farr, Elizabeth Anne Socolow, Michael Nethercott, and Patrick Dillon, who gave feedback on early drafts of this work.

My good colleagues Martin Lammon, Allen Gee, Laura Newbern, and Aubrey Hirsch.

Steve Heller, Hawaiian-shirted mensch.

My beautiful mother.

My sisters Ann and Clare.

My agent Christopher Rhodes – savvy, sensitive, stalwart.

Rhonda Hughes, intrepid publisher, superb editor.

Lidia Yuknavitch, for graciously providing an introduction.

The memory of my friend and swimming buddy Oliver Sacks.

And my brother George, who, as always, gets the last word.